The
Auschwitz Photographer

The Forgotten Story of
the WWII Prisoner Who
Documented Thousands of
Lost Souls

Luca Crippa and Maurizio Onnis
Translated from Italian by Jennifer Higgins

Published by Sourcebooks
P.O. Box 4410, Naperville, Illinois 60567-4410
(630) 961-3900
sourcebooks.com

Originally published as *Il fotografo di Auschwitz* in 2013 in Italy by Edizioni Piemme
S.p.a., an imprint of Mondadori Libri. This edition issued based on the hardcover *The
Auschwitz Photographer: Based on the True Story of Wilhelm Brasse Prisoner 4333* in 2021 in
Great Britain by Doubleday, an imprint of Transworld Publishers.

Library of Congress Cataloging-in-Publication Data is on file with the publisher.

Printed and bound in the United States of America.
SB 10 9 8 7 6 5 4 3 2 1

A Hedy Epstein, lei sa perché.
Alle migliaia di giovani che in questi anni ci hanno ascoltato
raccontare questa storia.

To Hedy Epstein, she knows why.
To the thousands of young people who, over the last few years,
have heard us tell this story.

Contents

For the sake of narrative and in service
to the translation from the original Italian,
some changes have been made to the timeline of events.

Auschwitz:
An Afternoon at the
Identification Service

WILHELM BRASSE SWITCHED ON THE ENLARGER, AND A bright beam of white light fell onto the sheet of photographic paper. The negative had been developed that morning by Franek Myszkowski, one of his colleagues, and Brasse hadn't even glanced at it. Myszkowski was a skilled lab technician, so Brasse was sure the negative would have the correct contrast and exposure. Brasse also knew his way around the enlarger, having worked with it for so long, and he was sure that with this medium-density negative, a dozen or so seconds of exposure would be enough to create the print. After exactly twelve seconds, he switched off the white light, and the room returned to semidarkness, illuminated only by the red safety lamp.

His boss, SS Oberscharführer Bernhard Walter, had asked

him to produce large prints, so Brasse had placed a thirty-by-forty-centimeter sheet of photographic paper on the base of the enlarger. Now he took the sheet—which already contained the secret of the image projected from the negative but was still invisible, still immaterial—and immersed it in the developing tank. He waited impatiently, as he always did at this stage of the operation, and the image slowly began to take form. It was a face; there could be no doubt about it.

First to emerge were the outlines of the eyes and a few darker strands of hair, then the features and the neck. A woman with a dark complexion. She was young and wore a scarf tied around her head.

When the pupils had become fully black, Brasse took the sheet out of the developer, rinsed it quickly, and submerged it in the tank of fixer: half a minute would be enough. He didn't even look at the timer sitting on the shelf next to him. This process had become second nature to him, and for a while now, he had no longer needed instruments to measure it. Finally, he extracted the sheet from the fixer, washed it carefully once more so the print wouldn't turn yellow, and hung it on a line to dry. He had asked Walter for a print dryer, but his superior was having trouble getting new equipment sent from Berlin. As for looking for one in Warsaw, there was no point: the Germans had already taken anything that could possibly be useful. Only after he'd hung up the print did Brasse switch the darkroom light back on. Standing there, in front of the line, he studied the image. He felt a surge of satisfaction: the print was perfectly developed and the contrast was just right. But that feeling quickly gave way to one of unease. The woman's eyes fixed him with a terrible gaze.

Disturbed, he took a step back to take a better look.

He wouldn't have been able to say from what distant country she came: the portrait was too close up for him to deduce anything from her clothes or other details. It was a face similar to the thousands of others he himself had immortalized here in the Erkennungsdienst—the camp's Identification Service. The woman could be French or Slovak, a Jew of any nationality—Romani even, although her features weren't like those of the nomads seen in Auschwitz. She could be German, punished for something the Nazis didn't like.

He didn't know.

The photograph had been taken by Walter, who didn't waste time explaining things. Brasse himself never went outside to take photographs. He had the authorization to do so but didn't want to. Unless they ordered him to do otherwise, he preferred to stay here, shut away in the warm studio, working alongside the other men in his kommando, as the SS called the various teams assigned to different tasks in the camp. Walter, on the other hand, liked taking photographs and producing short films out in the sunlight. He would then take everything back to the studio to be developed and printed.

The Oberscharführer appreciated and respected his chief portraitist, but he never failed to remind Brasse that he himself was an SS man and Brasse was a prisoner, worth less than zero.

Brasse's abilities were too useful to him, though, and with time, he had even developed a fondness for this Polish deportee. They chatted with each other, and Walter would ask Brasse's opinion on technical problems and entrust him with the most difficult jobs.

That morning, Walter had come into the studio early— before the queue of prisoners to identify and register had even formed—and when he appeared, everyone sprang to attention. The German had a roll of film in his hand, and judging by the care with which he was carrying it, it must have been something precious, and there was a lot of it—several meters.

"Where's Brasse?"

"In the darkroom," answered Tadek Brodka, who was preparing the equipment for the morning's work.

Walter crossed the room quickly and knocked on the door to the laboratory. He didn't want to barge in while the red light was on; he would have ruined his favorite prisoner's work. Only when he received permission to enter did he open the door.

"Good morning, Herr Brasse. How are you today?"

The photographer smiled at him. "As well as ever, Herr Oberscharführer. How can I help you?"

Walter held up the roll of film, then put it down on a table. "Here's some more work for you. When do you think you can develop it and get it printed?"

Brasse looked at the reel. "I'll start today, as soon as we've finished the registrations. May I ask what it is?"

Walter shrugged his shoulders. "Some pictures I took

yesterday as I was going around the camp. But they're very important to me, and they're for my superiors. Do you understand?"

The photographer understood perfectly. These pictures were
not destined for Walter's personal album; they would be seen by
the highest-ranking officers in the camp. He must work on them
with the greatest of care.

"Don't worry. Your prints will be perfect."

After this brief exchange, Walter had left and Brasse had gone
back to his usual tasks. He had worked on the reel in the afternoon,
and his prediction was confirmed. He produced perfect prints and
even cropped some of them to improve the Oberscharführer's
mediocre framing. And now here he was, looking at this woman's
face, allowing her gaze to fix upon him.

Her eyes were crying without shedding tears. The deep, black
pupils were full of terror and despair, wide open, staring. Lower
down, the curve of her lips betrayed how afraid the woman was.
She'd seen something—a dead body perhaps, or corpses being
piled one on top of the other.

Brasse realized immediately where and when the picture had
been taken.

The gas chamber. The woman was at the entrance to the gas
chamber. Perhaps she had watched the heavy doors opening or
closing and had seen inside, where they were clearing up after the
previous load. All this showed in her eyes: the fear, the horror, and
the tremendous realization that everything was about to end. That
she would be next.

Brasse shuddered.

He'd already seen many people die in the camp, but he had never seen eyes like this woman's: the eyes of someone alive but who, in a matter of moments, would meet their death. The eyes of someone who was watching the doors of hell open in front of them.

He moved away hastily and rushed to switch off the light. The darkroom fell back into a reddish gloom. The windows were closed, and he felt secure. As long as he was in there, nothing could happen to him.

He calmed down gradually and set about the day's work, registering prisoners for the Identification Service. He didn't want to fall behind.

PART ONE

Auschwitz, 1941: Hiding to Survive

I

"KEEP STILL! GOOD... DON'T LIFT YOUR CHIN TOO HIGH. Don't move... That's it."

The shutter clicked, and the prisoner's image was exposed onto the large six-by-twelve-centimeter negative. Brasse approached the revolving chair on which the prisoner was sitting. His subject drew back instinctively, as if he were afraid of being hit, but the photographer reassured him.

"It's all right. I just want to adjust something."

He neatened the collar of the man's uniform: one of the buttons was half undone.

Back behind the camera, he looked through the viewfinder again.

"Take your hat off and look straight at the lens. Don't blink, don't smile. No grimacing, please... What sort of a face is that?"

The prisoner couldn't hold his expression, even for the few seconds needed to take his picture. He was Polish and answered Brasse's question in their mother tongue.

"My back hurts. It's really bad."

The man who had escorted the prisoner to the studio was also a Pole. He was a kapo—a prisoner promoted to a position of authority in the camp—and he now approached the chair and gave the man a slap.

"Sit up straight and do what the photographer tells you. Here, all you do is obey!"

Brasse glanced at the kapo. He hadn't seen him before and didn't know which block he was from, but he wasn't afraid of him. Brasse was in charge in the studio, especially when it came to the "clients," and he didn't want prisoners to be needlessly mistreated.

"Kapo, don't hit him again! Not in my studio! Do you understand?"

The man swore under his breath and went back to lean against the wall. "All right, all right. But we'll deal with this disgusting rat later..."

Brasse repeated his requests to the prisoner, and the man finally looked at the lens, his forehead wrinkled, eyes wide, and neck straining with the effort of holding the pose. The shutter clicked.

When Brasse raised his head again, the prisoner hadn't moved. It had taken so long to get him into position that he was struggling to come back to reality. His eyes, still wide open, looked enormous in his emaciated face, and they were bright, so bright. In this moment, when he had forgotten everything, they gave a certain splendor to the rest of his face and his whole being. It was as if there were a stubborn flame deep within them that was determined not to be extinguished.

It was Brasse who broke the spell.

He reached out and pulled a nearby lever. Immediately, the prisoner's chair rotated ninety degrees, allowing him to be photographed in profile. But when Brasse looked in the viewfinder, he saw that the man, who had come to, was now too high up. Another lever lowered the chair, and finally the deportee's neck was at the right height.

"Don't put your hat back on. Look at the wall opposite you." The man obeyed, and the photographer took his final picture. "Good. You can go."

"Come on, walk!" shouted the kapo.

The man got to his feet with a look of disappointment. He wanted to savor the respite afforded by the photography process. He didn't want to go outside into the cold. He wanted to stay there, in the warmth. But there was no time. Another prisoner was ready to take his place. Already the queue was snaking out of the room. Brasse glanced over and saw at least twenty other prisoners waiting. They were standing up straight, not speaking, looking ahead. Not one of them dared infringe on the rule of total silence.

When one of them—perhaps the third in line—dared to sniff, the kapo exploded.

"Bastard! Disgusting animal! Jewish piece of shit!"

He began to punch and slap the man, first his body, then his face. His victim bent over, trying to shield his head with his arms and hands. He didn't dare react and only moaned quietly, almost in a whisper, but that was enough to send the kapo into a frenzy. The other prisoners moved away in terror. This had to be stopped, or the man would end up dead.

"I want him now!" Brasse pointed to the prisoner, who was now on the ground.

The kapo had to stop. He was panting, full of rage. "Why him? It's not his turn."

The photographer took the kapo's arm and drew him away from the group. He spoke to him politely, not wanting to make an enemy of him, but his tone was firm and carried the hint of a threat.

"Perhaps you didn't receive the order to bring the men from your kommando here to be photographed?"

"Of course I did."

"And who will be held responsible if we don't take the photographs?"

The kapo stared at him for a moment, his fists clenched. It was clear he would have gladly beaten up Brasse too. For all the photographer's airs, he was just another deportee, a louse. The kapo restrained himself, though.

"What do you mean?" he mumbled.

Brasse tried to speak even more politely. "My orders are

to photograph only those prisoners who look presentable. The pictures must be decent. I don't want beaten-up faces, black eyes, broken bones. I don't want suffering prisoners. My boss doesn't like that sort of thing. Do you understand?"

The kapo's lips tightened. He understood. He tried to stretch his mouth into a smile. "You won't tell your boss about this little incident, will you now?"

Brasse shook his head reassuringly. "I won't say anything. But let's photograph this man before the bruises appear on his face. Which kommando are you from?"

"We're from the garages. They're mechanics, and they're all settling in, getting too comfortable..." He snorted, as though it had fallen to him to reestablish discipline at Auschwitz, then barked at the prisoner he'd just assaulted to come into the studio and get on the revolving chair.

First shot: three-quarter view with cap. Second shot: full face, without cap.

Third shot: in profile, again without cap.

After each portrait, while Brasse worked on the framing, Tadek Brodka took the heavy case containing the negative out of the Zeiss to change it. Meanwhile, Stanisław Trałka composed written signs and placed them next to the prisoners so they would appear in the third picture. They detailed where each individual came from, their identity number, and why they were in Auschwitz. Brasse saw that the prisoner beaten up by the kapo was a "Pol S," a political prisoner from Slovenia, and that his identity number was 9835. Brasse calculated that this man must have arrived at the concentration camp a few months after him.

When Brasse had finished, he signaled to the prisoner that he could leave and caught a look of silent thanks in the man's eyes. The prisoner knew Brasse had saved him from a worse beating, but the photographer looked down and didn't respond. He had wanted to save this man from further punishment by intervening, knowing full well that if he had sent him away without taking his picture, there would have been a gap in the records. Ninety-nine times out of a hundred, the prisoners did not return for a second sitting. They were murdered before they had a chance.

Brasse had also been thinking of himself. Nobody knew what was going on in the Germans' minds, and he wouldn't have been surprised if he himself had been blamed for the missing photographs. He just wanted everything to run smoothly.

As the garage kapo pushed the next prisoner onto the revolving chair, Brasse glanced at the cuckoo clock on the studio wall. It was almost midday; soon the little bird would pop out of its door and sing. He found the sound annoying—it would always distract him at precisely the wrong moment—but he hadn't worked up the courage to ask the Germans to remove the clock. It amused Bernhard Walter, and that was enough. Another minute passed, the bird sang, and Brasse felt a strong pang of hunger and returned to the camera.

At that moment, Franz Maltz, the kapo of the photography studio, entered the room.

Brasse greeted him deferentially. "Welcome back, Kapo. Is it a beautiful morning outside?"

Maltz shook himself, trying to warm up, and went to stand next to the heater, covering it with his large behind. "Concentrate on your work, you Polish brute, and don't worry about me."

Brasse lowered his head without replying and looked through the Zeiss's viewfinder.

Nobody knew where the kapo spent most of his time, but it was clear he didn't understand the first thing about photography and could do nothing beyond producing a few copies in the darkroom. How he had become the Identification Service kapo was a mystery, but nobody dared ask him for an explanation. He was their direct superior, and that was all that mattered. He would often stand there next to the heater, eyeing Brasse as he made fine adjustments to the framing of a portrait.

A boy was now sitting on the chair.

He couldn't have been more than eighteen, and Brasse felt his throat tighten as he studied him. He wore the yellow triangle on his chest, with a red one sewn over it to form the Star of David. He, too, was Jewish and would certainly not live long, but it was not this that stirred Brasse's compassion. It was the boy's gaze. His eyes were pale and clear, with the trusting look of a youth only just past puberty.

Freckles peppered his face, his eyelashes were long, almost feminine, and his demeanor was gentle. There wasn't a hint of facial hair on his cheeks or chin. Brasse felt sure that no insult would ever pass this boy's lips. He would die calling out to his mother, staring at his executioners, stunned, without understanding why they were killing him. He probably had about two weeks to live. Work, cold, hunger, and beatings: it was only a matter of time.

As soon as the third photograph was taken, Maltz shouted, "*Weg!*"

It was the German order to get lost, beat it.

The boy was French and presumably didn't understand German, but he understood the curt tone of the command and tried to get up as quickly as he could. It wasn't fast enough.

His feet weren't yet on the ground when the garage kapo pushed the lever next to the desk, causing the chair to turn quickly back to its original position. The boy was thrown to the ground like a doll, hitting his face on the edge of the platform on which the Zeiss stood.

As he lay on the ground immobile, Brasse felt the impulse to assist the boy, but it was forbidden to help deportees, and he would have gotten into trouble. So while Maltz laughed madly, the Jewish boy got up with difficulty. Once he was on his feet again, the garage kapo shoved him out the door, laughing. This little game was new to him, and he was enjoying it enormously.

"Very good! Shall we do it again?" he said to Maltz.

Maltz, who was still doubled over, managed to reply, "Did you see the look on his face? I could die laughing! They're so upset... Oh God, his face. So upset... Yes, let's do it again!"

The revolving chair threw three more prisoners to the ground.

One in particular—an old man—broke his arm as he fell. He lay on the ground, crying out in pain and fear. In pain because his arm was bent into an unnatural position and in fear because he knew this incident would mean the end for him. He would be taken straight from the studio to the hospital and from there to the crematorium. Nobody had any interest in feeding and caring for an old man. The sooner he was out of the way, the better.

All this—the broken arm, the fear in the man's eyes, the chaos created in the studio—increased the two kapos' hilarity all the more. They didn't stop to catch their breath for several minutes, but then Maltz regained his habitual frown. He had let off some steam and didn't want to joke anymore.

He stretched and yawned. "I'm going to buy something to eat. Do you want anything?"

He sniggered, knowing full well that Brasse and the others working in the studio didn't have money to spend. He left them alone to deal with the prisoners.

Brasse looked at the cuckoo clock. It was nearly one o'clock. His hunger pangs were intensifying, but he would have to wait. They still had many hours of work ahead of them.

2

IT HAD ALL BEGUN A MONTH BEFORE—FEBRUARY 15, 1941, the day they'd sent him to the Political Department, after the first terrible winter spent in Auschwitz. On his walk over, Brasse noticed that he wasn't alone: four other prisoners were also looking for the SS building. As they trudged through the snow in their clogs, their arms wrapped around their chests to keep in the meager amount of warmth produced by their famished bodies, the men exchanged a few worried remarks, wondering why they had been singled out.

"Where are you from?"

"France. And you?"

"Holland."

"I'm from Slovakia."

"I don't understand…"

Only Brasse spoke German, so to make themselves understood, the four other men used the few words they had learned in the Babel of the camp, communicating as much through gestures as through language.

They came from different countries and were different ages: two were over fifty, one was thirty-five, and the other two—including Brasse—were younger still. There seemed to be no link between the prisoners or their kapos; they worked in different kommandos and slept in different blocks. They grasped for ideas. Then something occurred to Brasse.

"What were you registered as?"

The others looked at him, puzzled. "What do you mean?"

"What did you do before you came here?" he replied impatiently. "What did you say to the SS?"

"I was a photographer," said the Frenchman.

"Really? What about you?" Brasse asked, turning to the Slovak.

The man nodded. "I was a photographer as well. I had a studio near Bratislava."

The Dutch and Hungarian men confirmed they too had been photographers.

"And me," said Brasse. "Do you know what that means?"

The five men slowed to a halt, taking care not to slip on the ice. The door of the Political Department was a few steps away. They looked at one another without resentment but with a little suspicion. A few seconds had been enough for them to realize that, for a reason as yet unknown to them, the Germans needed a photographer—perhaps two. But not five, surely. So this was going to be a selection process.

Brasse broke the silence and tension that divided them.

"Come on. Let's go. The Germans decide everything anyway."

They entered the building cautiously, each one asking permission to step inside before giving his name and registration number.

"Present!" they almost shouted in loud, clear voices, as though their destinies depended on seeming more disciplined than their companions.

The men were made to wait, standing up, with no explanation, while each in turn went into a small room. The murmur of voices inside could just be heard. When the interviews were over, each man was taken outside through a back door. The five were never all together again. They weren't able to exchange even a glance, and an SS man with his bayonet raised made sure they couldn't tell one another what had happened inside the room.

When his turn came, Brasse found himself in front of a desk that took up almost the whole room. There was hardly any space left for the man sitting behind it: an Oberscharführer, or SS senior squad leader. A man on whom Brasse's life might now depend. The photographer's heart was in his mouth. He was about to repeat his name and number when the Oberscharführer signaled that he should remain silent.

"Please sit down, Brasse."

Brasse looked at him, astonished. It had been many months since anybody had used the word *please* with him. He clutched his cap in his hands and took a seat. "Yes, sir."

The German, a young man of about thirty with a pleasant face, scrutinized a few documents. He then began to ask a long series of questions, patiently, without hurrying, as if getting to the bottom of this matter was of vital importance to him.

"I see from your papers that you're twenty-three years old and you used to be a photographer in Katowice."

"Yes, with my uncle."

"Did the studio belong to him?"

"To my aunt, but my uncle worked there. I was his apprentice. I learned the profession well."

"How well?"

The officer was smiling, and Brasse was tempted to go on, but he realized he would pay dearly for any exaggeration—passing himself off as the best photographer in Poland would be useless and dangerous. He stuck to the truth.

"Very well." He wasn't lying. He really was good.

"What do you use for developing?"

"Agfa liquid… The German one is better quality than any of the others," he said without irony.

"And for the fixing?"

"Agfa for that too."

"How do you go about retouching?"

Brasse wondered where all these questions were leading.

They obviously needed a photographer, one who could do darkroom work, but retouching was something else. It was what you did with portrait work, in city studios, in the upmarket areas. He didn't understand.

"I did a lot of retouching with my uncle, but you need the right tools..."

"Such as?"

Brasse glanced around uncertainly, as if to suggest that Auschwitz wasn't the kind of place where you'd find such things.

"You need pencils of different grades, glossy and opaque black inks, soot, emulsion. And lots of other items. That's the only way to do proper retouching."

The Oberscharführer gave a satisfied nod. He seemed pleased by what he'd heard. He shuffled the papers once more, then opened a drawer, took out a small photograph the size of a postcard, and showed it to Brasse. It was of a figure in civilian dress, an old man unknown to Brasse. The half-length portrait had almost certainly been done in a studio, but it was not perfect.

"What do you think of this picture?"

"It's not quite right," Brasse answered honestly.

"Why?"

"The three-quarter pose is good, as is the expression on the face, but the right-hand side of the face is too much in shadow. There's a problem with the way it's been set up."

The German leaned toward him. "Go on."

"The lamps aren't positioned correctly. Or perhaps the

photographer didn't have enough light sources. It could do with another lamp to lessen the shadows on the man's right cheek. That's the problem."

The Oberscharführer looked at the photograph. "That's my father, and I took the picture myself."

Brasse swallowed but didn't reply, frightened now.

"I took it at his home in Fürth, in Bavaria—my hometown. I only had the lamps in the living room. For an amateur, it isn't bad, don't you think, Herr Brasse?"

He emphasized the *Herr*, and Brasse felt faint, but he had the presence of mind to reply.

"Yes, for something done with only what was available in the room, it's a good photo."

The German nodded. "Yes, it's a good photo, but I'm too busy to spend all my time on photography." He looked down again at the documents on the desk and wrote something on them with a few decisive strokes.

Those are my papers, thought Brasse, full of anguished anticipation.

The Oberscharführer finished writing and handed him a sheet of paper. "These are your orders. The Slovak knows more about photography than any of you, and the Frenchman isn't bad either, but you, Brasse, have an advantage over them. Or rather two advantages…"

Brasse remained silent.

"The first is that you speak German, and I don't want to have to communicate with gestures, like a monkey. I'd have to do that with them. The second advantage is that you—despite the fact that you insist on declaring yourself to be Polish—are the son and nephew of Austrians. It's my duty to pay special attention to Aryans. Even those who deny that status."

Brasse blushed at this, and the German noticed. He gave an unpleasant smile.

"The camp is a hard master, and perhaps with time, you may want to join us. The Wehrmacht is certainly more welcoming than Auschwitz, and our uniform is far superior to the striped one that you prisoners wear. Don't you think?"

"That is certainly the case, sir."

"Good. Now go."

Brasse didn't move.

The officer's brow furrowed immediately. He waited for a moment before blurting, "Are you already disobeying me? I told you to get out!"

"Excuse me, sir. What work have you recruited me for?"

The officer struck his forehead with his hand. "I nearly forgot! My name is Bernhard Walter, and as of today, I'm your new boss. You are part of the Erkennungsdienst—the camp Identification Service. Our job is to take photos of the prisoners and archive them. Everyone who comes into Auschwitz must pass in front of your camera to be registered. You begin in one hour. Is that clear?"

"Yes, sir."

"Now go."

Brasse bowed briefly and left the room.

The SS soldier saw him out and left him standing alone in the snow, trembling with joy. In the most unexpected way, a light had appeared at the end of the tunnel. Almost unable to believe what was happening to him, Brasse did a little jig, there in the cold. Then, shaking more and more as the adrenaline drained from his body, he made his way back to his barracks. He was crying, and never had his tears seemed so sweet.

3

"What have we got this morning?"

It was half past six, and the members of the Identification Service kommando were already in the darkroom in Block 26, with the obvious exception of kapo Franz Maltz, who always took his time and arrived very late. He claimed that being on time was no fun, and they understood the reason why: Walter had ordered him not to beat any of the prisoners in his team, so Maltz had decided he might as well leave them alone to work.

"What have we got this morning?" Brasse repeated.

Tadek Brodka's reply came from inside a store cupboard where all the garbage from the laboratory was piled up higgledy-piggledy.

"Just a minute. Here I am."

Brodka emerged from the cupboard on all fours and stood

up, holding a parcel wrapped in old paper. He opened it to reveal a loaf of black bread and a large lump of margarine. "The cook gave them to me in the kitchen yesterday, in return for the enlargement of the photo of his wife."

The men didn't wait to hear his explanation. It was winter, it was cold, and they were hungry. The cupboard also doubled as their secret larder, and in recent weeks, it had often remained empty. Despite all the "favors" that could be had in the camp, getting ahold of contraband food was still difficult and dangerous. If Maltz—or, even worse, Walter—found out, nobody would have been able to save them. Now, though, they were desperate to eat, and there was no use worrying. Brasse reached out and touched the bread, then shook his head.

"Hard as rock. Will you sort it out, Stanisław?"

Stanisław Trałka nodded. He took the loaf and made his way to the big guillotine they used to crop the photographs. In a few seconds, the knobbly bread had been sliced and distributed across the improvised table. The margarine, too, was divided into portions.

Wilhelm Brasse, Tadek Brodka, Stanisław Trałka, and Władysław Wawrzyniak ate their breakfast and, for a while, enjoyed not only the food but also the peace of this meal, taken together among friends, before getting down to work.

"Let's not eat it all. Keep a piece for Franek and one for Alfred."

Franek Myszkowski and Alfred Wojcicki were the other two

members of the kommando. Myszkowski was currently in the hospital with a bad case of bronchitis from which they all hoped he would recover quickly. They were confident that he would—his skill in the darkroom was so vital to the Germans that they looked after him as though he were one of their own. Wojcicki was in the studio, pretending to tidy and dust the equipment. In reality, he had a very different job. Just then, he burst into the darkroom.

"Quick!" he said anxiously. "Maltz is coming."

The men jumped up, mouths full, and within a few seconds were all at their posts. The bread and margarine disappeared back into the cupboard, where only a very careful search would reveal them. Only a spy could have discovered the men's secret, and they knew that none of them would tell. They had to trust one another if they wanted to survive.

Brasse immersed himself in his work and barely heard Maltz shouting and swearing. He usually spent the first part of the morning, until ten o'clock, printing the photographs taken the previous day, and to do this, he shut himself away in the darkroom, isolated from the rest of the world.

The group worked like a well-oiled machine. During each sitting, Brasse took the pictures, aided by Brodka and Trałka. Meanwhile, in the darkroom, Wojcicki, Myszkowski, and Wawrzyniak worked on the negatives removed from the Zeiss after each shot. The tanks in which they submerged them could contain as many as thirty negatives at a time. After half an hour, they removed them, rinsed them, immersed them in the fixer, and rinsed them again. Finally, they hung up the negatives to dry. It was only at this point that Brasse took over.

In the morning and after five o'clock in the afternoon when the last deportee had been registered, it was his job to turn the negatives into photographs. He rarely produced contact prints directly from the photographic film, preferring to enlarge the pictures first, knowing that the Germans wanted decent-sized identity photographs. He was performing this very task on this particular morning while the others cleaned the studio and prepared the developing equipment.

Printing the images was a complex task, and he couldn't rush it.

He also couldn't allow himself to fall behind. His photographs went to the Political Department, where they were put into the prisoners' files. They were vital for identifying the deportees: the Germans wanted to be sure they were murdering the right people. Brasse was obliged to stay in the darkroom until late in the evening to finish his work, going out into the square for the roll call and then returning to Block 26, with Walter's permission, until midnight or one o'clock in the morning. The following day, he would be exhausted, but it was still better than digging in the freezing cold of the gravel quarry or making bricks for new camp buildings.

There was only one way of getting the job done any faster: being less careful, less precise with the exposure of the negative, or making smaller enlargements. He could have stopped retouching the photographs altogether, but he did this work in secret, using pencils that Myszkowski had obtained for him, and he did it out of respect for the prisoners. They were the living dead, and he wanted to present them to history with their dignity intact, so he spent hours correcting shadows or softening angular features. Evidence of kicks and punches were visible, especially in the enlargements, so Brasse removed them. One day in the future, somebody would find these images, and Brasse wanted that person to know that these were men and women, not animals.

He was lost in these thoughts when Maltz opened the door of the darkroom without knocking first. The kapo knew this would ruin the prints, but he didn't care. It was his way of reminding the members of the kommando—and Brasse in particular—that although he couldn't touch them, he was still the one calling the shots.

"It's ten o'clock," he barked. "The prisoners are waiting. Go!"

Brasse made his way into the studio and set to work.

The first subject on the list was a slightly fleshy, well-groomed man who must have been a doctor or a lawyer, certainly some kind of professional. Then there was a little old man with frightened eyes and sunken cheeks. He was so short that they had to raise the chair as high as it would go to get him into the frame, and his legs were so shaky that Brasse couldn't understand why the Germans had let him live this long. Perhaps he was doing some kind of important work for them; there was no other explanation for it. The third prisoner, in a grotesque contrast that made Maltz snigger, was a beanpole of a man, about forty years old. He was both extremely tall and extremely thin and was all the more gangly because each day spent in Auschwitz made him even more skeletal. After the man's sitting, Brasse paused for a moment.

"Where are they from?" he asked his fellow workers.

"I heard they're from Block 11," replied Trałka, who was busy composing the identification signs.

Brasse shuddered. If they were from Block 11, then their kapo must also be in the corridor. A fellow Pole, Wacek Ruski was feared by all and considered one of the worst beasts in the whole camp.

Brasse looked out of the studio, and his anxiety increased. It took him only a few seconds to realize that some of the individuals standing in the queue were people he knew from Żywiec, the town where he was born and raised.

There were three of them—Wachsberger, Springut, and Schwarz. He hadn't actually been friends with them, but he knew them well because Wachsberger ran a pub near the station and the other two were shopkeepers: one was a pharmacist, and the other ran a clothes shop. The number of times Brasse or his mother had greeted them in the street! The number of times he had gone into the pharmacy on some errand or other, or his mother had bought offcuts of cloth from Schwarz!

The sudden memory of his mother, of his home and his town, made Brasse's legs tremble, but he soon managed to chase these thoughts from his mind. The ability to do so—not thinking about the past, not thinking about the future, but living in an eternal present and not looking beyond it—was essential to survival. At this moment, though, here was his past, barging in to meet him. And to make it worse, these three men, despite their Aryan names, were Jews. They would soon be dead, he knew.

All this passed through Brasse's mind while Ruski's shouts slowly filtered into his consciousness. The kapo never once stopped terrorizing the men from his block with insults, and if any of them made even the slightest move to pull away, he brought his stick down on their heads, knocking them to the ground like oxen in a slaughterhouse. Brasse hated him, not for the violence but because he was a Pole who was betraying his people. He was a Polish kapo who enjoyed beating Poles.

Brasse plucked up his courage and approached him.

"Wacek, listen. Let me give these three men a cigarette…"

The kapo looked at him malevolently. "Fuck off!"

"Look." Brasse pulled a packet of ten cigarettes out of his pocket. "I'll give one to each of them, and the other seven I'll give to you. All right?"

Ruski smirked. Without replying, he held out his hand eagerly to grab the cigarettes. Then he turned to the wall, pretending not to see.

Brasse made his way over to the three men from Żywiec, who only now looked up and recognized him. He saw amazement and happiness in their eyes, and he smiled warmly at them. They couldn't speak to one another, but there was no need to. He gave them the cigarettes and lit them. They inhaled with joy, and their faces relaxed. For a moment, even for these three Polish Jews, the old times seemed to have returned, when all was well and life went on peacefully.

Wachsberger, the pub owner, winked at Brasse.

"When all this is over, you can come and have a meal on the house," he whispered so that Ruski wouldn't hear him.

Then, counting on the fact that Ruski was now deep in conversation with Maltz, Brasse pulled up the jacket of his uniform and put his hand into a secret pocket in his trousers where he always kept something to eat. He took out a hunk of bread and offered a piece to each of his three acquaintances. They opened their eyes wide and put the food in their mouths, swallowing it without even chewing. They knew it would give them enough energy to survive one more day.

Schwarz, who was the oldest, held out his hand to Brasse. He wanted to shake hands and embrace the younger man but was overcome with shyness. With eyes full of tears, he only managed to stammer, "Thank you! You're a good boy!"

The photographer wanted to cry too, but he couldn't. If Maltz had caught sight of him, he would have demanded an explanation, and it would have ended badly for the three. Instead, Brasse gave them a silent salute and turned back the way he had come.

As he reached Ruski and Maltz, he hesitated for a moment, then decided to speak.

"Wacek, I want to ask something of you."

The Pole gave him a menacing look. "What do you think you're doing, interrupting a conversation between your superiors?"

"Please, listen to me."

"Listen to him," said Maltz sarcastically. "Our artist always has some favor or other to ask. Just try to get as much out of him as you can." He went off, laughing, while Ruski looked at Brasse resentfully.

"Well, what do you want?"

Brasse pointed to the three men.

"Wacek, please, if you have to murder them… If you have to kill those three Jews, kill them so they don't suffer."

"Are you mad? I'll kill them however I like!"

"Please, Wacek, I haven't got anything to give you in exchange for this favor, but I beg you, don't make those three suffer."

The kapo, his forehead furrowed in an effort to understand such an unreasonable request, didn't reply and remained silent for a long time. Then he whispered furiously, "I don't take orders from anyone! Not even you!"

"Please, Wacek."

But Wacek turned his back on him and began bellowing at his deportees.

A little later, Brasse photographed Wachsberger, Springut, and Schwarz. Like hundreds of others, their faces materialized in front of the lens of the Zeiss only to disappear again, and there was no more mute communication between them. He watched them disappear into the corridor, their shoulders drooping and their steps hesitant, as the door of the studio closed behind them.

Only later on, after five o'clock, did Brasse's thoughts return to the three Jews from Żywiec, and his heart felt constricted. His mind dwelled on his mother, father, and brothers, about whose fate he knew nothing at all, and also on the hopefulness of the past that was now dead. He had asked a murderer to kill kindly. Brasse was a rational individual, capable of reflection, who respected and loved life, but he had asked a murderer to kill.

To kill kindly, but to kill nonetheless.

He waited for news of the deaths of Wachsberger, Springut, and Schwarz for several days, wondering whether Ruski had listened to his plea. He knew about the kapo's favorite method of murdering prisoners. He would knock them to the ground on their backs and position the handle of a shovel across their necks. Then he would stand on it, but not with all his weight. Just enough to suffocate them, little by little, killing them slowly. This was what Brasse had asked him not to do.

Less than a week later, Brasse heard that all three men were dead: shot with a pistol up against the wall of Block 11. He never knew whether it was a coincidence or whether Ruski had remembered his plea, but either way, the Jews from his town hadn't suffered. His sense of guilt was lessened slightly.

Asking someone to kill wasn't always a sin.

4

THE DAY THAT BRASSE PHOTOGRAPHED THE MEN FROM Żywiec seemed never-ending.

A few minutes after eight in the evening, just after roll call, Oberscharführer Walter came running over to Block 26. Seeing the studio was empty, he opened the door to the darkroom and poked his head around it. Brasse was at work inside, and he looked up with a frown, thinking that it was yet another of Maltz's idiotic intrusions. However, when he saw Walter's black SS uniform, he jumped to his feet, cap in hand.

"Call the others," Walter ordered. "You'll be working all through the night tonight."

The officer disappeared swiftly, leaving Brasse no time to ask questions.

The photographer rushed outside, along the short dirt track to Block 25, and summoned the Identification Service kommando. Then he sent Alfred Wojcicki to fetch Maltz. The Germans slept apart from the rest of the work team, and Wojcicki later confessed to Brasse that he'd been worried Maltz would vent his anger at being roused on him. Instead, the kapo spared Wojcicki but beat a cook who happening to be passing near Block 13, leaving him half-dead.

The men were soon ready to get down to work but found themselves alone in the Erkennungsdienst. Brasse switched on the lamps and checked that the light was angled correctly toward the revolving chair. Brodka inserted a new negative into the Zeiss, and Trałka prepared a couple of identification signs: he was certain they would be doing at least one "asocial" (as the Nazis termed those imprisoned for not fitting their narrow definition of society) or Romani, or perhaps a Slovenian. The others mixed fixing and developing solutions, but for a good half hour, nothing happened. After a while, they ended up falling asleep with their heads resting on the desks or in their chairs.

Brasse was the first to wake up, roused by the whistle of a train: a convoy had arrived. Before he could wake the others, some loud shouts from Walter did the job for him.

"On your feet! Get ready to work!"

It wasn't long before the silence of the night was broken by the sound of footsteps, faint at first, then louder and more intrusive. *It's like a hailstorm*, thought Brasse, except it was a storm of people. He watched his companions looking at the windows, the walls, the roof, with fear in their eyes, trying to understand what was happening in the darkness outside.

The footsteps grew deafening and continued to be accompanied by the kapo's angry shouts in German. Finally, they came to a halt outside the door to the Identification Service. Maltz opened it, and the new "guests" at the camp began to file in. Walter himself was there to welcome them and give them instructions, which had never happened before. He was behaving like a host.

Brasse went over to him.

"Herr Oberscharführer, can you tell me how many there are? Then we can work out how fast we need to work."

Walter replied without even glancing at him.

"Work as quickly and as accurately as you can. A transport of eleven hundred Jews has arrived from Rotterdam, and we have selected just over two hundred of them. They'll be here shortly, Brasse, and my superiors want them all registered before tomorrow morning, understood?"

Brasse could have objected, saying that photographing two hundred deportees in one night was impossible, but there was no use. He was dead tired after his long day, and he didn't know if he would be able to hold out until the morning, but he would have to if he wanted to avoid going back to the Russian roulette of camp life. He followed his orders, and as the first Jew took his seat in the revolving chair, Brasse bent over the camera. Immediately, he raised his head in amazement.

The prisoners were wearing civilian clothes. It was obvious, now that he thought about it, given that they'd only just arrived, but this had never happened before. He went back to the viewfinder and observed the man in front of him. He was around forty, not very tall and a little plump, and wore a jacket, trousers, and a heavy wool coat. Under the jacket was a stained white shirt buttoned up to his chin; he'd obviously suffered from the cold on the journey. The man followed Brasse's instructions to reposition himself, but before the shutter clicked, he said, in German, "One moment!"

He looked down at his shirt, embarrassed by the stains, then turned to the photographer, as if asking him what to do. Brasse motioned to him to button up his jacket to hide the dirt as much as possible, and the man complied. He adjusted his round glasses and his thinning hair and held on to the peaked velvet cap in his hands.

The man was—and still felt himself to be—an ordinary civilian, not a deportee. The camp had not yet dehumanized him. He was finding the Erkennungsdienst procedure normal, reasonable, and even reassuring. Nobody would waste time photographing and registering him only to kill him afterward, would they?

Brasse took the picture, and that was the first one done.

A long stream of men and women followed—all well-dressed, even elegant. They were exhausted after their long journey in the cattle cars but were already managing to regain their dignity. None of them knew what was ahead of them, and this ignorance made them "normal," almost beautiful, to Brasse.

It soothed his spirit, and the pictures from that night were among the best he had taken in Auschwitz. Naturally, he tried not to ask himself how many of the eleven hundred Dutch Jews that Walter had mentioned would survive their time in the camp. Undoubtedly, he would have been able to count them on the fingers of one hand.

Toward three in the morning, the kommando had photographed about half of the prisoners, and Brasse stopped for a break. He went out into the corridor, yawning and stretching, and found Maltz there. He was working with a few colleagues and two or three Jews from the Effektenkammer, the place where goods taken from new arrivals were stored. Maltz and the others were grabbing suitcases and bags from the prisoners, opening them up and choosing what to keep and what to discard. The deportees didn't dare protest, confident that surely they would get back their clothes, medicine, and toiletries at least. They patiently endured the Germans' shouts and slaps.

Just as Brasse was about to go back into the studio, he was stopped by a man wearing a fur coat. The stranger checked that the guards weren't looking, then removed his wide-brimmed hat. He turned it over to reveal precious stones, diamonds, and all sorts of jewelry hidden inside.

"Take them!" he urged Brasse. "They'll last you the rest of your life! But help me get out of here!"

The man's eyes were penetrating and his tone authoritative. He must have been used to giving orders in civilian life and hadn't yet understood the trick that fate had played on him. He was desperate but also animated by a cast-iron will to survive. He pushed the hat against Brasse's chest.

"Take it, I tell you! And help me!"

The photographer stepped back and looked at the man. He could see out of the corner of his eye that neither Maltz nor the other kapos were watching him, but the idea of taking the jewels didn't occur to him even for a second. There was nothing he could do to help this man, and he didn't want to accept his jewels. Anyway, this kind of thing always led to trouble. It was one thing getting his hands on a piece of bread here and there to ward off starvation, but it was another thing to get involved in something of this scale. If he took the jewels, he knew it would end badly for him.

He pushed the hat away.

"I can't. Give them to someone else."

And he returned to the studio.

When the man in the fur coat appeared in front of the camera, he was no longer wearing his hat, and Brasse was sure he must have offered the jewels to one of the kapos. He was just as sure it had been a futile gesture. That man would be struck down like all the others by hunger, beatings, and hard work.

After all, he was Jewish. For him, there was no hope.

That night, plenty of other riches went up in smoke.

Toward dawn, Myszkowski appeared at Brasse's side. He had been outside in the corridor. He showed Brasse a roll of banknotes—they were hundred-dollar bills, and there must have been thousands of them.

"I found them in a suitcase," he said. "What should I do?"

Brasse looked at his friend. He was excited and worried at the same time.

"Burn them!" he replied and pointed to the stove.

Myszkowski looked from Brasse to the money and from the money to the stove. The color drained from his face. He was clearly tempted to keep these riches for himself. If he was clever and lucky, they could guarantee him a long life, even here in Auschwitz.

"Burn them, I said!"

Myszkowski looked at Brasse and made his decision. He threw the roll into the fire.

Then he returned to the darkroom with Brasse, and the pair set to work again.

By seven in the morning, the kommando had photographed and registered each and every one of the two hundred or so prisoners from the night convoy.

They had worked well, and Bernhard Walter was pleased with his kommando.

5

WILHELM BRASSE, ON THE OTHER HAND, WAS AFRAID.

He had good reason to be very happy with his new life. He was a little king in Block 26—he ran the studio and the darkroom expertly, his abilities were recognized by his superiors, and as long as he obeyed orders and everything ran smoothly, he realized that, thanks to his talents, he was surrounded by an invisible aura. He was untouchable, and this gave him the courage to keep going. However, he was also aware that any of the Germans, be they SS or kapos, could kill him on a whim and wouldn't be punished for it. His existence still hung by a thread, and he couldn't shake off the fear.

His first months at Auschwitz had marked him indelibly, and he could forget nothing of what had happened during that time.

The faces of dead companions constantly returned to his mind, and he often had to blink repeatedly as he looked at prisoners through the viewfinder of the Zeiss. They sometimes seemed to have taken on the faces of the priests that the infamous kapo Ernst Krankemann had tied to a heavy roller used for construction work and then thrashed to death in September. They'd arrived at the camp at the same time as him and had been killed straightaway. He would see their eyes again, their tears, and would wait in terror, fearing that at any moment, they might ask him for help. Then he would shake himself and return to work: a three-quarter shot with the cap on, one full face, and one in profile. Dozens of them, hundreds of them.

His fear also led him to avoid being seen around the camp.

Every morning, he was woken at half past five, and he made the most of the warmth of Block 25. They had heaters there, a sink with running water, and a flushing toilet. He could wash, sip the bowl of slop they called coffee in peace, and think about the day's work ahead. With him in Block 25 were the other men from the Erkennungsdienst and many other privileged prisoners who worked with the Germans in the kitchens, the uniforms department, the stables, or the administrative departments. All of them were doing all right and didn't complain.

Whenever he left Block 25, Brasse kept his head down, but first he would glance around quickly to make sure he wasn't about to cross paths with any of his superiors. If he could, he would walk the few meters to Block 26 without once lifting his eyes. He didn't want to see anybody's face, didn't want to see anything at all. If he were to raise his eyes, he was sure to see something awful: a kapo beating a prisoner; a deportee standing in the snow as punishment; a sick person dragging themselves along, waiting for the final blow that would finish them off. The less he saw, the less he would remember.

He would then make his way into Block 26 and immerse himself in the Identification Service work from early in the morning until late in the evening. He dedicated himself to it completely, with every fiber of his will, using all the skill he had learned in Katowice and all the creativity he possessed. He never looked out the windows; it helped that he spent long hours shut up in the darkroom. In Auschwitz, being able to take refuge in an enclosed room with no view of the camp outside, of real life, was an invaluable piece of good fortune.

That morning, when he crossed the threshold into the studio, he found Stanisław Trałka sitting at the photography desk with a pen in his hand and a sheet of paper in front of him. When there weren't any Germans around, Trałka used the desk for writing. He was a literature student and had told Brasse that he'd been arrested by the Wehrmacht in November 1939 while he was in the university's faculty building. That day, the Nazis had rounded up dozens of professors and a good few students as well: the cream of the Polish intelligentsia. Trałka had arrived at Auschwitz from Tarnów prison, just like Brasse, but some time before him. He was one of the camp's earliest arrivals: his number was 660.

His work today was certainly not a piece of literary criticism.

"Listen," he said to Brasse.

"What is it?"

"A letter to my family."

Brasse frowned. "How do you think you'll get it out? You've already tried a couple of times."

"Lacek, the plumber, is sure he's found a guard who's ready to turn a blind eye."

The photographer shrugged. He didn't approve of this sort of intrigue. If the Germans found the letter, they would beat up the guard and kill Trałka, and it would be a bad business for the whole of the Block 26 kommando. He couldn't stop men feeling nostalgia for home, though. Trałka was even younger than Brasse himself and had left behind his family and fiancée in Kraków.

Brasse sighed and nodded to Trałka to read out the letter.

"I've just started, and I'm telling them about our lives."

"You're mad."

Trałka laughed. "Don't worry. I'm hardly saying anything. They'd think I'd gone crazy and wouldn't believe me. I'm just talking about normal things so they won't worry. Here we go: 'We all come from different parts of Poland, but in the photography studio, we've become a sort of family. We spend most of our time here: we work, eat, chat about all sorts of things, and sometimes cook, competing to see who's the best.'"

"We cook, do we?" asked Brasse sarcastically.

Trałka shrugged. "No. But we'd like to, wouldn't we?"

"Go on."

"'We only go back to our barracks to sleep, and thank God we each have our own bunk with a straw mattress. The wake-up call is at five thirty—too early, especially for me. As you know, at home I never used to get up before seven, and before a hard day's work, I could do with more sleep, but it's not possible here. You have to toe the line, and if you're late for roll call, you're in trouble. Still, the night is the best part of our lives in the camp because we're free to dream about whatever we like. Nobody, not even the Germans, has yet found a way of controlling my dreams, and I often dream of seeing you all again. It's a wonderful, sad dream, because it makes me think I'm at home again, free.'"

Trałka looked up from the letter and met Brasse's eyes.

"That's as far as I've gotten. What do you think?"

"You're lucky. I never dream about being free."

"Do you want to die here in Auschwitz, my friend?"

The photographer was unable to reply.

A quiet whistle came from outside: a sign that another member of the group was arriving and, more importantly, that there were Germans about. Trałka hid his paper and pen and immediately set to work. A few seconds later, Alfred Wojcicki came in, followed by Maltz, who was in his usual foul mood. The kapo shivered with cold, spat out something that had gotten stuck between his teeth at breakfast, and went straight to the stove to light it. He wouldn't move for at least a quarter of an hour, until he was nice and warm.

The morning passed peacefully, between work in the dark-room and the studio. For the first time, the only "clients" coming into the Identification Service were women.

"Where have they come from?" asked Tadek Brodka in surprise.

Until then, they had photographed female prisoners very rarely. As far as Brasse and his team knew, Auschwitz wasn't the women's ultimate destination. But rumors in the camp spread quickly, and they had heard recently that a new women's section with five or six barracks had been opened in the Birkenau area. Seeing so many of them lining up there, waiting for their identity photographs, could only mean one thing: those barracks were full and their occupants had come to the slaughterhouse, ready to go through the camp's deadly machine.

Brasse could hardly bring himself to look at the women.

He'd been taught that war was a game between men. Even in Auschwitz, that was the case. He maintained this belief when he saw all those Slovak, Dutch, Czech, and French men and all the others who appeared in his viewfinder. He knew there were victims and executioners, and he felt himself to be a victim, but he consoled himself with the thought that it had always been this way, for thousands of years, between men. The Romans hadn't treated the barbarians very kindly, and Genghis Khan was crueler even than the Germans. But at least they were all men. These subjects before him were women; they had nothing to do with war, and he couldn't understand why they were in the studio. His job had become a hundred times more painful. He couldn't keep his eyes on them. He would have liked to close his eyes and never open them again.

He forced himself to look.

A young girl sat before him: Yugoslavian, according to the sign prepared by Trałka. She had the round, open face of a country girl. She was shapely, and even the striped uniform couldn't hide her femininity. She wore her headscarf tied at the nape of her neck, and when she took it off for the second and third photographs, her hair fell down to her shoulders. It was filthy, a detail that moved Brasse because of the contrast with his mother's hair, which was always thick and shining. The Nazis deprived the women of Auschwitz the thing that counted above all for them: the right to take care of their bodies.

For the first time since he had been assigned to this kommando, Brasse wanted to know more about the subject of his photograph. He looked around. Maltz was nowhere to be seen.

"What's your name?" he asked the girl in German.

"Jacina."

She didn't seem surprised by Brasse's familiarity.

"Why are you in the camp?"

The girl glanced around in turn and replied in a careful, barely audible whisper.

"I was a partisan dispatch rider. They got me and brought me here."

This simple piece of information astounded Brasse. He asked, almost stupidly, "There are people resisting the Germans?"

She didn't answer but nodded.

The photographer was seized by frustration and annoyance. He couldn't approach the prisoners without permission under the best of circumstances, still less so if they were women. He wanted to say something or do something for her, but he didn't know what. When the Birkenau kapo took the girl away, Brasse remained caught between action and inaction, between saying something and holding his tongue.

At that moment, Maltz came back into the studio. "Close your mouth, Brasse!"

"What?"

"Close your mouth, idiot! You've got it open like a dead fish." Then Maltz smiled mockingly and added, "Seeing women gets you like that, does it? Well, it's to be expected. You're young."

Brasse didn't reply. He closed his mouth and turned his attention back to the Zeiss.

After the Yugoslavian came a much older Jewish woman who, curiously, was trying to look as poised as she could. She tied her headscarf under her chin carefully, tidied her hair, and bit her lips to make them brighter. Next was an unfriendly looking German woman with hard, unpleasant eyes. *She'll end up being a kapo*, thought Brasse. Then a Slovenian political prisoner of about twenty years old: a girl with fine features but small, evasive eyes. A Dutch woman was next, then another Jew. All women, victims of a men's war.

When, after an hour, Brasse paused to look up, he realized

that Brodka and Trałka were holding handkerchiefs against their noses, and their faces were twisted into expressions of disgust. Maltz had disappeared, which was strange, because he was always on the lookout for women and had always hung around while they were being registered. He would stand next to the photography table, watching them, looking at their figures under the uniforms, and it was clear that, given the chance, he would have raped them all. But at the moment, which could have been a triumphant one for his bestial desires, he was nowhere to be seen.

Brasse noticed Brodka and Trałka seizing the opportunity for a break to remove the handkerchiefs. They shook their heads and went into the darkroom. He opened the door of the studio and glanced down the corridor. Dozens of women were standing there waiting their turn. Only one female kapo was guarding them, and she was standing immobile near a window. She, too, had a handkerchief over her nose.

Brasse finally understood what was wrong.

The air was filled with the heavy, stifling odor of bodies that hadn't been washed for weeks. It was unbearable and seized him by the throat, forcing him back into the studio. Until then, he'd been so immersed in his work that he hadn't taken any notice of it, but it was the women who were the source of this stench.

Every delicate thought about femininity was chased from his mind, and it was difficult to get back to work. From that moment on, his only wish was that the queue would shorten as quickly as possible. A few times, he didn't bother moving the lamps to get a better shot, and he stopped asking his subjects to soften their expression. He just wanted to get it done and for the women to go.

Finally, a little after six, the stream of prisoners came to an end, and the men of the kommando threw open the doors and windows. They had to let some air into the studio and the laboratory, even if it meant letting in the chill of the evening. "Do you know why they're like that?" Brasse asked Brodka with a grimace.

"They don't have water."

"What do you mean?"

"There's no water where they're kept, either in the barracks or outside. They can't wash."

"Are you joking?"

His friend looked at him, annoyed. "Of course I'm not joking. A man from a barracks near to Birkenau told me. The smell from the women's block reaches all the way over to them. He's already worried about what it'll be like in summer. He thinks the stench will be even worse."

"But what about their...?"

"Their what?"

"Their times of the month... Their cycle..."

Tadek Brodka shook his head, laughing loudly. "That's just about the only thing they don't have to worry about."

"Why?"

"They've found out that nature works with the Germans. What with the hunger, the beatings, and the cold, they stop menstruating. They don't have periods anymore. Interesting, isn't it?"

Brasse gagged and turned to look out the darkroom window. The sky above Auschwitz was clear, and the crisp, dusk air helped him recover. Things never stopped getting worse, and he couldn't come to terms with it.

He interrupted his own train of thought.

He remembered that he should never look out the window; he shouldn't look at the world outside.

But he had, and it had been a mistake.

6

BLOCK 20 STOOD A FEW METERS IN FRONT OF BRASSE.
It was where the Nazis kept prisoners struck down with typhus,
and one of its windows almost directly faced the one Brasse was
looking out in the darkroom. An SS officer was walking up and
down the length of the room, talking and gesticulating, as if he
were angry with someone there.

Brasse didn't know the name of this man with the skull
symbol on his cap. He'd known him by sight for a long time but
had never tried to find out more. He didn't want to gather information on him, and in any case, it made no difference to him
whether the man's name was Funk or Seler or Bruder.

During the day, the man was elsewhere in the barracks

building, hidden in some other room, but at this time in the late afternoon, he was always there, in the space revealed by the window facing the Identification Service.

He was always holding a syringe in his hand.

He would lift it up against the light—perhaps this was why he chose this room, as it got the most sunlight—and then point it downward.

Once, twice, three times. Dozens of times each afternoon, with slow, measured movements. The work was punctuated with chatter, laughter, arguments, and curses. Sometimes the officer's face was relaxed, sometimes it was scrunched up, and Brasse could tell whether he was enjoying his work at that moment or hating it. It was like watching a silent film without subtitles.

There was nothing to indicate what might be in the syringe.

On that particular day, after a few minutes, the photographer looked away to his left, toward the entrance to Block 20.

There were several young men standing in a row, waiting their turn in silence. They weren't far away, and he could see the Star of David sewn onto their jackets. Who could say what they had been told? Today, the Nazis had chosen young adolescents; they couldn't be more than fourteen or fifteen.

"Do you know where they've come from?"

Wojcicki, who had come into the darkroom to prepare the tanks of developer for the following day, came up to the window and looked outside.

"I think they're Greek. At least that's what they're saying in the kitchen. Apparently, one of the boys asked if he could have some tzatziki. They're still laughing about it."

Brasse could see that the death factory was working with perfect efficiency.

The boys went into one end of Block 20 alive and came out corpses at the other end.

In the evening, like every evening, the workers would come with their carts to collect the bodies. It was one of the things that Brasse tried not to see when he was returning to his barracks.

Now he couldn't help watching the SS man in the room of Block 20.

He might have a syringe in his hand, but he wasn't wearing a white coat. He wasn't a doctor. Learning to murder with a needle was something any Nazi could do. It was easy to get the hang of it, even if they weren't a doctor or a nurse. It only needed a corporal or any troop sergeant. Not even an officer.

A quarter of an hour passed, and the lights in the room in Block 20 went out suddenly. Brasse could no longer see anything except the young Greek Jews still waiting in silence at the entrance.

The SS man had vanished. Brasse closed the window and turned to the enlarger, trying to concentrate on his work. He had dozens of portraits of women to print. Foolishly, he wished he had a proper background in the studio, perhaps one with a rural landscape on it. He could have put it behind the women to soften the images.

He had just dipped a print into the fixer when someone knocked at the door. He jumped.

"Who is it?"

"It's me, Herr Brasse. Your neighbor."

He didn't recognize the voice but quickly put two and two together.

What did this man want? He had never come to the Identification Service before, and he had no reason to be here now, because any request to work with them had to go via Bernhard Walter.

Brasse was seized with panic. Suddenly, this demon had materialized before him, and he couldn't send him away by telling him that he was too busy or by spinning some other lie. Trying to be smart with an SS officer was a crazy thing to do. He turned on the white light and cleared his throat.

"Come in!" he called. "The door is always open to my superiors!"

The man entered the darkroom and introduced himself politely.

He was young, perhaps the same age as Brasse, and he was holding his black cap in his hand, as though he were the prisoner and Brasse the German. He seemed embarrassed and lacked the authoritative air of most of the Nazis in the camp.

He looked around him attentively, examining the equipment in the darkroom: the enlarger, the developing and fixing tanks, the packets of light-sensitive paper. It was all top-quality material that Walter had sourced from Warsaw or had had sent from Germany. The SS man let out a whistle of admiration.

"How may I help you?" Brasse asked.

The man looked at the photographer again and smiled.

"I need to ask a favor of you, with Oberscharführer Walter's permission."

Brasse made sure that his face betrayed no emotion, but he felt very disturbed by this intrusion. And he was worried, because the man in front of him seemed like the most courteous person you could imagine. It didn't make any sense. He nodded at his visitor, encouraging him to continue.

The German extracted a small picture from his pocket and handed it to the photographer.

"Oberscharführer Walter himself took this picture a few days ago. It's of me at work. I want to keep it for myself, but I also want to send a copy to some of the boys I used to work with. They're in France, lucky devils—in a garrison. And I got sent here… Do you think that would be possible?"

Brasse took the picture without looking at it, put it on the table, and nodded.

"Certainly. You can come and collect it in a couple of days."

The man smiled again in childish pleasure, revealing shining white teeth, then backed obsequiously toward the door.

"Thank you. You're very kind. I'll tell Oberscharführer Walter that you've been a great help to me."

Only when his back touched the door did the German turn around to feel for the handle, and he didn't leave before he had saluted Brasse. The door closed behind him.

Alone again, Brasse closed his eyes and waited for his heart to stop pounding. He passed his hand over his forehead, which was beaded with sweat, and tried to calm down. The photograph lay on the table in front of him, facedown.

He waited for a long time before reaching out to pick it up. Eventually, he took it by one corner with the tips of his fingers, as you might touch a venomous insect. Then he turned it over.

The man had been photographed in his uniform with an ax in his hand, chopping up a large tree trunk. Brasse could tell it had been taken on one of the construction sites around the camp. Standing close by were the carpenters who would then use the wood to make a roof beam.

It was an innocent photograph—a simple, everyday scene of manual labor.

No evidence of the systematic crimes to which the SS man dedicated his afternoons.

Better that way.

Brasse sighed and looked up from the image, hearing lively voices coming from the studio. The German, before returning to his barracks, had stopped to chat with the men from the Identification Service. It would seem the kommando had made themselves a new friend.

He put the little photograph down on the table. He would copy it tomorrow.

He got to his feet and went to the window to look over at Block 20.

The room opposite was dark and empty.

And the Greek boys were still there, at the door, patiently waiting their turn.

7

JUST AFTER FIVE O'CLOCK THAT AFTERNOON, KAPO
Maltz poked his head through the laboratory door and barked an
order.

"Come here. There's a skin job for you!"

Brasse didn't say a word but switched off the white light,
took the six-by-twelve negative out of the enlarger, turned off the
machine, and made his way through to the studio. A "skin job" was
a job for Dr. Entress. Brasse didn't know this doctor personally,
but he knew about his passion: tattoos. He had heard that Entress
also conducted surgical and chemical experiments, but within
the Identification Service, he was known only for his interest in
tattoos. Of any kind.

As soon as a prisoner with decorated skin arrived, Entress

would send him straight to Block 26. Butterflies, sailors, scantily clad women, birds, daggers, skulls and crossbones—over the last few months, Brasse had photographed dozens of tattoos. Entress would then ask a laborer to collect the pictures.

That evening, Brasse found himself confronted with a tall man of about forty, in his prime, with thick black hair. He had obviously only just arrived at the camp; otherwise, he wouldn't have been looking around with such an obviously lofty gaze.

"Go on, salute the photographer!"

Maltz accompanied his invitation with a mighty kick to the man's backside and a scornful guffaw. The man didn't move, though. It was as if he were made of stone. He looked at his persecutor with fire in his eyes. His hands were trembling, and he was clearly on the verge of attacking the kapo.

Franz Maltz was also big and beefy, but he must have had enough of arguing that day, or perhaps he wasn't as stupid as he seemed. He spat on the prisoner's uniform and swore.

"I'll leave him to you," he concluded and left the studio.

When he was gone, Brasse spoke to the deportee in German.

"Where are you from?"

"Gdańsk."

"Are you Polish?"

"Yes. That's why they sent me here."

The pair immediately switched to their native tongue, and the photographer lit a cigarette for the man in the hope that it would encourage him to talk. It turned out that his name was Karol and he'd been a stoker. *The perfect job with those muscles*, thought Brasse. After Gdańsk became occupied in 1939, he had managed all right for himself, but then things had grown complicated.

"I was working on ships around the world," Karol began, "and I hardly ever came back to Poland, except for a few days at a time to load up with goods and coal. We barely even realized there was a war on. I was always on the boat, and the Nazis weren't crazy enough to stick their noses into my boiler room. That carried on for two years. Then they got serious."

"What do you mean?"

"One day, they ordered all the Polish sailors on ships in the port to come ashore. Gdańsk is German now, and they wanted me to change nationality—to become German. Nazi, to boot. They wanted to send me to the front. They beat me to try to persuade me, but I said no. We'll see if I did the right thing."

Brasse revealed that the same thing had happened to him. He, too, had refused to fight for the Nazis, the crime of his refusal aggravated by the Aryan blood that ran in his veins. So the two men were both in Auschwitz for the same reason, and neither knew if they would come out alive. He then asked Karol if he knew why he'd been sent to the Erkennungsdienst, but the man shook his head.

Brasse smiled. "It doesn't matter. I know. You're a skin job for Dr. Entress."

The man frowned. "I'm what? And who is Dr. Entress?"

"A doctor with a particular passion. Take off your jacket."

The stoker removed the jacket of his uniform, and Brasse saw that his chest and arms were free of tattoos.

"Take off your trousers and underpants."

When the man hesitated, Brasse waved away his concerns.

"Don't worry. It's nothing strange."

The man didn't have any decorations on his groin or legs either. Eventually, Brasse asked him to turn around, and it was then he saw the tattoo Entress was interested in. He gave a cry of admiration and called out to his kommando.

"Hey, come here! You don't want to miss this."

The rest of the Erkennungsdienst stopped what they were doing and crowded around the photography desk. Brasse was right. Before them stood the best subject for a photograph they'd ever seen in Block 26.

"You're a living work of art, my friend!" cried Wawrzyniak, saying out loud what they'd all been thinking.

Karol's whole back was covered in a colorful tattoo. The scene was the Garden of Eden, and it depicted the most famous story in the whole of Genesis. On the left, Adam was holding the forbidden apple in his hand. In the center, the serpent twisted itself around the tree of the knowledge of good and evil and offered a second apple to Adam. On the right, Eve was looking at Adam. She, too, had an apple in her hand.

"I don't think he'll be able to resist. Three apples is too many," Brasse said out loud, though he'd only meant the thought for himself.

"True," said Myszkowski, "and it's his fault we've all ended up in Auschwitz."

This joke was received with bitter laughter, all the more so because it expressed a truth. Terrible things were seen every day in the camp, and if man had deserved them through some original sin, it must have been an awful sin indeed. If God was still punishing them for Adam and Eve's behavior, he wasn't showing any sign of being satisfied yet. Perhaps he would keep them in this hell for ever.

"Have you seen the look she's giving him?"

The tattoo really was beautiful, full of precise, refined detail such as the snake's scales and Eve's hair. The colors were rich and bright, in a palette dominated by reds and blues. But all this artistry didn't obscure the sensuality of the scene, and nothing expressed it better than Eve's gaze, lustful and full of desire for her man.

"Who did it, Karol?"

"A man in Valencia, a couple of years ago. It's good, isn't it?"

"Very," said Brasse. "Now we need to take a picture of it."

The stoker laughed. "Is this your Dr. Entress's passion?"

"Yes. And we obey his orders, even though it isn't always easy."

The studio was equipped for taking portraits and nothing else. Brasse feared the day he would be asked to take a group shot, because even with all his skill, he wouldn't be able to make up for the studio's shortcomings. Even the stoker's broad back was going to pose some difficulties. The revolving chair and the Zeiss were both fixed to the ground so that the shots were always framed correctly, and he couldn't move them. The only way to photograph this man would be to get him to sit astride the chair with his back to the camera.

Brasse moved the lamps so that as much light as possible fell on his subject. Then, to be sure of getting the best shot he could, he took three separate series of photographs in different lights. The whole operation took over an hour. When they had finished, Brasse heaved a sigh of relief.

"That's it. You can get dressed."

"Thank goodness."

The studio was heated but the stoker had grown cold staying in the same position for so long. He began to sneeze—once, twice, three times.

Before he left, he smoked another cigarette, with obvious enjoyment. He told Brasse today was the first time he'd had any since arriving at the camp.

"Don't you smoke?" he asked the photographer, puzzled.

"No, but I like giving them away," Brasse admitted. "It helps people who come here to feel better."

The stoker looked around him. His expression was easy to read: it was warm inside and he didn't want to leave. The Identification Service kommando had a good setup. He knew he had no choice, though.

"What does your doctor do with all the tattoo pictures?"

Brasse looked at him uncertainly. "I don't know. I think he files them away. Perhaps he uses them for his research."

"Ah," grunted the prisoner. He smoked the cigarette down

until it almost burned his fingers. "You're good people," he said before he finally went outside. "Goodbye."

Brasse watched him for a minute, only going back into the studio when he saw the man turn the corner and disappear into the night. The photographer felt uneasy, because he hadn't been entirely truthful. It was true that he didn't know what Entress did with the photographs, and he didn't understand why on earth he was so interested in tattoos. Anyone could see they had no scientific value at all. Even so, despite the fact that Maltz appeared fairly regularly with a new "skin job," Brasse had never wanted to ask why. That was his rule: never to ask about anything that happened outside the Identification Service.

The answer to any questions he might have had about Entress came to him eventually, at a time when he hadn't thought about Karol for a long time. He wasn't looking for this answer and didn't want it, but there wasn't a single corner of Auschwitz that didn't stink of death: it permeated the entire camp.

About six weeks after Brasse had photographed the stoker, a friend of his from Kraków, Mieczysław Morawa, sent word to say he had something interesting to show him. Brasse pretended not to have received the message, because Morawa worked in the crematorium, and Brasse had had enough of that place, having been forced to spend his first terrible months at Auschwitz there, unloading the bodies of the dead. But Morawa insisted, adding that his friend should hurry—he wanted to show him something really extraordinary.

So it was that one morning, before beginning his printing work, Brasse got onto one of the carts belonging to the Leichenträgerkommando—the corpse transport work team—and traveled to the crematorium, worried but also glad for a breath of fresh air. When he saw Morawa, he hugged him with joy. It had been weeks since they'd seen each other, and it was good to confirm that they were both still alive.

"Come with me. I'm sure you'll be interested in this."

Morawa walked past the ovens as his coworkers fed the fire with new corpses, never once pausing in their work. The two men went right to the end of the crematorium and stopped next to a table. Something lay stretched out on it. Morawa took Brasse's arm.

"You know what that is, don't you? I wanted to show you so that someone else besides me could witness it. If I'm lucky enough to get out of here alive, I'll tell all about this, but I know that nobody will believe me, so I wanted you to see it too. We need to have enough people to tell the story."

Brasse saw Karol's back on the table. It was held down by weights at the edges and seemed in good condition.

His knees began to tremble. He tried to say something, but his voice caught in his throat. He could only speak after several attempts. "Who did this?"

His friend didn't reply. He lowered his eyes in silence.

The photographer, in shock, thought about what it must have been like to have to skin a man. He leaned over and vomited on the ground.

Morawa held him up and pulled him away, out of the crematorium.

"Was it Entress who told you to cut the tattoo off this man?" Brasse pressed.

"Yes. He came in person."

"What did he say to you?"

Morawa looked him straight in the eyes. "He told me to treat the skin carefully and preserve it well, because it's going to be used as the binding for a book. He said that. And he repeated it. Do you understand? A man died because a mad doctor wants to bind a book. What do you think is so precious about the book?"

Brasse didn't answer this impossible question but staggered away. It was a long walk back to the Erkennungsdienst, but he needed some time to calm down and think.

Yes, a man had died because some crazy doctor wanted to bind a book with his skin. It was true. Karol, the stoker from Gdańsk, had been shot or strangled or hanged—it was impossible to say—because Entress wanted a beautiful addition to his library. It had happened, there was no doubt of it, but Brasse couldn't find a place in his head for this insanity. He hadn't yet been driven mad enough to entertain this reality: it was too big for him, and he wanted to stay sane as long as possible. He wondered if it was necessary to attain a certain level of madness if one was to survive in Auschwitz. The answer was yes, there was a minimum level, and he needed to reach it if he wanted to survive.

As he was walking, it occurred to him that Entress worked

in Block 7, where his patients were. The thought seized him to go there and see what Entress looked like. He considered it for a long time as he stood in the middle of nowhere, at risk of being beaten up by a kapo or an SS man for wandering about aimlessly.

Then he decided that Entress's face didn't interest him. If he saw it, it would be stuck in his mind forever. It was better to go back to the Identification Service, close the door behind him, and bury himself in the laboratory work. He had a mountain of negatives to print and turn into photographs.

That was his only task.

8

THE CHAOS IN BLOCK 26 THAT MORNING WAS INDESCRIBABLE.
Two days earlier, the kommando's clerk had been taken ill, and
Władysław Wawrzyniak had been appointed in his place. Wawrzyniak,
who usually worked in the darkroom, wasn't proving to be a good
replacement and had made a mistake summoning prisoners to be
photographed. At ten o'clock, there were two rows of inmates queuing
up, one of women and one of men. The deportees were silent and
motionless, fearful of arousing their persecutors' anger, and the kapos
were arguing about who should have their photographs taken first.

Brasse went out into the corridor and bellowed at them.
"Quiet! This is what we'll do: we'll take a woman and then a man,
then a woman, then a man, alternating between the two lines. That
way, you'll all lose less time. All right?"

The guards stared at him blankly, silent at last. Then, after half a minute or so, they began to argue again, as though he hadn't even spoken.

"Shall I call Oberscharführer Walter?" he threatened.

It was enough to bring them to their senses, and Brasse nodded in satisfaction.

"We'll do as I suggest. Bring in the first person."

First in line was a stout young man who barely fit into his uniform. That morning, he had asked for a bigger size, and his request had cost him a black eye. With his visible injuries, Brasse had no choice but to send him away. Then came a middle-aged woman. She was Jewish, with blond, wavy hair and a gaze that lit up Brasse's viewfinder. It was the look of a mother who would not allow herself to be broken, who would endure anything simply because she has no other option: before giving in, she must save sons and daughters, brothers and sisters, a husband and a father. This determination helped to keep some mothers alive, even in Auschwitz. Brasse smiled at her, grateful for this glimpse of goodness, albeit a silent one.

Then came the turn of a boy, a Dutch political prisoner. No matter how much Brasse asked him to, the boy couldn't manage to look into the lens. In his full-face picture, he kept his eyes stubbornly lowered. Brasse was ready to shout at him but he held back; he didn't want the kapo to beat the youth with his stick, so instead he took a photograph that he knew wasn't perfect. It was the first time he'd done so since he'd begun work for the

Identification Service, and he'd manage to justify himself some way or another.

When it was the next person's turn—a Czech woman—pandemonium broke out in the corridor once more. Annoyed, Brasse rushed out to see what was going on.

Two kapos, a man and a woman, were rolling about on the ground, locked together and fighting to the sound of shouts of encouragement from the other kapos. Meanwhile, a young girl was lying facedown on the floor, her hands covering her bloodied face. When Brasse opened the door, everyone turned to look at him, like children caught stealing candy. The kapos got to their feet, and the silence that followed was broken only by the girl's faint whimpers.

"What happened?"

"We don't owe you any explanations, you piece of shit," said the man who'd been in the fight.

Brasse realized with horror that it was none other than Wacek Ruski.

"He hit one of our prisoners," said the woman Ruski had been fighting, trying to justify herself.

"Why?"

"I only stroked her, and she gave me a nasty look, that's why!"

"Liar! We know exactly where you stroke them! You had your hand between her legs."

While the kapos continued arguing, Brasse looked at the object of their dispute. The injured girl couldn't have been more than fourteen and seemed so fragile that it was hard to believe

Ruski's claims. This weak little thing would never have challenged a madman like Ruski, even with a look. When she had managed to get up, Brasse pointed at her.

"Bring her in."

Hesitantly, the girl came into the studio and sat in, or rather climbed onto, the revolving chair. She was like a frightened bird, and her haphazardly shaved hair gave her the look of a bald, newborn chick.

Brasse approached the seat. "What's your name?"

"Czesława."

"Are you Polish, like me?"

She nodded.

"Why are you here?"

"They arrested my father and my whole family, but we didn't do anything."

Her eyes filled with tears, and she had to force herself not to cry. It was obvious she didn't want to attract the guards' attention and get hit again.

"Don't worry now. We'll take the pictures, and then you can go back to your block in peace."

The girl sniffed and put her headscarf back on, tying it in a big bow at the nape of her neck. Then, with the sleeve of her uniform, she wiped the blood from her lips where Ruski had hit her. She even tried to smile—it was as if having her picture taken had transported her back to her childhood days—but she couldn't quite manage it.

Brasse looked at her through the viewfinder. With her huge, shapeless uniform that hung off her body and her headscarf over her forehead, she looked like a little boy, and he felt a rush of tenderness toward her. It wasn't fair that fate had dealt such a cruel hand to such an innocent creature. Brasse bit his lip—now it was his turn to stop the tears from coming. He swallowed, asked Czesława to keep still, and took the photograph. Then he took her by the hand and walked her out of the studio. He hoped that one day, after the war, some family member or friend would find Czesława's portrait in the camp archives so that she, too, would be remembered. She wouldn't have died for nothing.

Just then, Maltz came in.

"Tadek, get outside! Walter and Hofmann need you!"

Brodka glanced over at Brasse, who nodded his assent.

"Tell Alfred to come out of the darkroom and give me a hand," the photographer told his assistant. "Come back as soon as you can."

"All right."

Brodka called to Wojcicki to take his place by the Zeiss, picked up a small portable camera with a viewfinder on top, and followed Maltz outside. This kind of summons was not unusual. Walter and Hofmann, the Oberscharführer's subordinate, often wanted to have pictures taken of camp life, and they would ask Brodka to help them. In fact, Brodka had a very specific job.

More than an hour passed before Brodka returned to the studio. Brasse didn't say anything to him but watched as his assistant went back to his usual post at the photography desk in silence, his eyes lowered. He set to work mechanically and remained there until late in the afternoon, when the two queues of prisoners had finally disappeared.

It was just after five o'clock. Only now did Brasse speak. "How many today?"

"Two."

"Where?"

"One hanged himself in Block 12, and the other threw himself on the electric fence. I gave the film to Myszkowski to be developed on my way back. I hope it's ready. Walter and Hofmann want to see the photographs this evening."

Brasse calculated the time they would need to get the prints done and grew worried.

"Walter also wants the album of photos I printed on Wednesday ready today. How do they expect us to get all this work done?"

Brodka shrugged his shoulders. It wasn't his problem, and it wasn't up to him to solve it. Brasse didn't resent his attitude. This young man, known mockingly outside their block as the "suicide photographer," had spent a long time among prisoners, SS men, and kapos that morning, and he was still upset by the sights he had witnessed.

"Were they young?"

"One, yes. The one who hanged himself."

"Who's in Block 12?"

"They're from all over Europe. He did it last night. He tore his uniform into strips and hanged himself from a beam. They found him before roll call and left him there until we arrived. They told me he was from Belgium and that he'd just turned twenty-five."

"Two years older than me," Brasse interrupted him.

"And three years older than me."

"Nobody noticed what was happening?"

"Nobody. Or at least that's what they say. I'm sure the others in his bunk must have seen and heard it, but if they say anything, they're in trouble for not having stopped him or called the kapo. Walter says the same thing, even though he doesn't actually care either way. He just wanted me to take the pictures. He made me take a whole roll, from every possible angle. He even brought two SS battery lamps because it was so dark in the barracks you couldn't see a thing."

Brodka paused, lost in thought, before adding, "He had a peaceful look on his face, though, the man who died. If he did suffer, he must have comforted himself with the thought that it was all about to be over."

"What about the other one?"

Brodka sniggered.

"The other one was cunning. More cunning than any of us!"

"What do you mean?"

Brodka lit a cigarette. It helped him remember better. He smoked all the cigarettes he managed to get his hands on—as many as ten a day—and nobody knew where he got them from.

He said that smoking was the only thing that calmed him down and helped him cope with the tension.

"He was about fifty. He'd just gotten off the train. He thought that men his age would all be murdered, but that didn't actually happen. He'd gotten through the selection process and was being marched over to the barracks, but he already understood how it works here. He was cleverer than us. And braver..."

"Why do you say that? Do you think we're cowards, just because we want to live?"

Brodka gestured with his arm, his cigarette tracing a semicircle in the air.

"He didn't wait until he'd reached the very bottom. We delude ourselves. We think we'll save ourselves, but we won't. We'll touch the bottom one day, and that day, we'll discover that we haven't even got the strength to kill ourselves."

Brasse didn't answer. He was angry. He wasn't a coward. He was just trying to scrape along and get by somehow. That wasn't a sin.

He walked away, trying to banish these thoughts from his mind, and went to find Myszkowski. He wanted the negatives of the day's suicides—he had to print them straightaway. They were ready, but before beginning his task in the darkroom, he made his way over to Wawrzyniak, who was sitting at a table in the studio, working away peacefully.

Wawrzyniak had arrived at Auschwitz from Kraków at the beginning of 1941, having been caught by the Germans during a street raid. He wasn't a particularly expert technician, and Brasse had needed to teach him most things, but the SS had selected him to work in the Identification Service for a different reason: he was skilled in calligraphy and wrote beautiful captions in gothic script for the pictures in the albums ordered by the Germans. Brasse printed the photographs, then they told Wawrzyniak the order in which the images should be placed and what he should write underneath.

The SS worked on the photographs with great precision, noting the place, date, and time of each one. What they did with these albums was a mystery. They certainly weren't intended to be presented to Reich officials as evidence of the work carried out by the men in black uniforms—far more detailed statistics were needed for that. The most likely explanation was that Walter and his bosses presented them to high-ranking officials visiting Auschwitz.

For a few minutes, Brasse watched in admiration as his colleague traced elegant curlicues under the photographs with a fine pen and cobalt-blue ink. Then he told him to take a break.

"Go and have something to eat in the darkroom, Władysław. You haven't had a bit to eat since this morning."

Wawrzyniak looked at him doubtfully.

"But I've still got lots to do…"

"Go on! Walter won't be here for another couple of hours, and Maltz isn't around. Nobody will find out if you have a break. I'll stay here and keep watch."

Wawrzyniak gave him a grateful smile and got up from his chair.

Brasse took his place. He wanted to spend a few minutes alone studying these photographs, which he himself had printed a few evenings earlier. Ever since he had seen the crude black-and-white images emerging from the developing tank, he hadn't been able to rid his mind of the stories that the pictures told.

He'd heard a lot of things from other prisoners about the Auschwitz selection process. When he'd arrived at the camp, the system hadn't yet been perfected: there were no gas chambers at that point, and he and those who arrived with him had simply been unloaded more or less in the countryside and then taken over to the barracks. The Germans had soon become more organized, and all sorts of rumors reached the Identification Service about the way in which the SS chose which prisoners to kill and which to save and about the way in which the first unfortunate group was murdered. Brasse was familiar with the crematorium, but he'd never seen the gas chambers. Not close up. And he had never witnessed a selection.

Until that point, the men of the Erkennungsdienst had only produced albums for Walter in which he and his friends were the main focus: scenes showing the SS men's lives in the camp, during their time off, or on holiday in Warsaw. Sometimes the albums showed prisoners working and chronicled the construction and enlargement of Auschwitz. However, a few days earlier, Walter had presented them with a set of very different images, documenting the arrival of a convoy, the selection process, and what happened afterward. Walter had taken them all himself and had worked with the tenacity of a reporter.

The largest photograph, on the first page, was a crowd scene: thousands of people who had just gotten off the train. Men, women, and children all mingling together. People searching for other people and families trying to stay together. In the middle of them all, SS men and kapos were already separating people and beating them with sticks, shouting at them to go here or there. In the background, Brasse noticed with a shiver something that had escaped him in the darkroom: a column of thick, black smoke rising toward the sky. It wasn't coming from the train. It was from the crematorium, which worked day and night, a familiar landmark to all the camp's prisoners. In the foreground was a woman with a white scarf wrapped around her head, holding a newborn baby. She had her back to an SS man who was pointing at her, as though he wanted to give her an order and she was already getting away. Walter must have climbed up on something to have taken an image with such a wide angle. A stepladder, perhaps, or the bucket of a bulldozer.

Many other images followed that first one. There were people organized into orderly queues as they got off the train and waited for the doctors and officials to decide who would be saved and who would not. Mothers in headscarves, with enormous Stars of David on their chests. Men in overcoats, grasping the handles of their suitcases tightly, as if holding on to the few possessions brought from home would reassure them that everything was all right, that all this was normal. Women and children were separated from husbands and fathers.

There were three young boys at the front of one picture. The oldest, a teenager, looked disoriented as he held the hands of the two younger ones, who were still cheerful. The women, meanwhile, couldn't understand what was happening and were staring anxiously at the camera. Men walked toward the barracks, unaware that they had just escaped death, without their suitcases now. And there in another photograph was a mountain of luggage: a kommando of prisoners was opening the bags, large and small, and scattering the contents around them. The first thing they looked for, Brasse knew, was money and jewelry. Only later would they sort clothes, toiletries, kitchen utensils, books, and newspapers. And so on.

Oberscharführer Walter's photographs showed a normal day of arrivals at Auschwitz. All except the last one. The gaze of the woman that had made such an impression on Brasse in the darkroom. Those black eyes were still there, clinging to life, staring implacably at him. He noticed that Walter had instructed Wawrzyniak to place this image at the very end of the album. So Brasse had guessed correctly: the woman was taking her final steps toward death, taking her final look at the world before the darkness. Wawrzyniak had not written the caption yet, but Walter's instruction was there. It read, "Jew going to the gas chamber. Auschwitz, September 30, 1941, 4:30 p.m."

Brasse closed his eyes and put the album back on the table. He was horrified, and shivers ran up his spine.

No matter how hard he tried to avoid it, the outside world kept on knocking at his door. He did his best to isolate himself, but the more he tried, the more reality invaded his life. He knew it was useless to hide away.

He wanted to be alone, but in Auschwitz, that was impossible. Sooner or later, he was sure, reality would come and ask him to settle his debts.

And he would have to pay up, all at once.

PART TWO

Auschwitz, 1942–43: Serving the Master

9

"PLEASE SIT DOWN, HERR BRASSE."

The photographer twisted his cap uneasily in his hands and gave a little bow of thanks before taking a seat in the front row. He barely had time to look around and wonder who would be sitting in the other five or six rows of chairs that filled the room. Nobody, apparently, because Walter sat next to him and signaled to the projectionist, who turned off the lights and plunged the room into darkness. As the projector whirred to life, images began to appear on the wall in front of them. They had all been taken outside, in the camp.

Brasse shifted apprehensively in his seat. The film was shoddily produced, with haphazard framing and ragged black edges, and he wondered which incompetent could possibly have been responsible. Usually, he and his team developed the SS's films, but in this case, the kommando had been kept out of the process.

"I sent this to Warsaw to be developed. It's very sensitive material," Walter explained, as though reading Brasse's mind.

Brasse's unease grew. The Hauptscharführer—Walter had recently been promoted—was showing him raw, unpolished footage, and yet he had summoned him to the Political Department expressly for that purpose. Brasse hadn't set foot in there since the day he'd been taken on as part of the Erkennungsdienst more than a year earlier, and things had changed dramatically in the meantime. The Political Department had moved from the old barracks building and was now in Block 13, where it took up a whole floor. Now the men in black uniforms had enough space to work, and Walter had even managed to set up a little projection room, where he presumably showed the fruits of his art to friends. But these details weren't what was unsettling Brasse; rather, it was Walter's friendliness in inviting him and arranging a special private showing.

The images went by quickly. Brasse watched prisoners gathering for roll call and answering when their names were called, leaving their barracks in the morning and returning in the evening, working in the SS vegetable gardens and building their houses, and digging supply and drainage channels for clean and dirty water. He didn't ask any questions, and only after a few minutes did he notice one particularly odd detail: this film had been made in warm weather, but they were now in the midst of winter. In this celluloid world, there was no snow on the ground, the Germans were in summer uniforms, and the prisoners weren't stamping their feet to keep warm.

He hazarded a comment. "This is an old film, sir."

"I made it last September. Do you remember last September, Brasse?"

The photographer turned his mind away from the images to focus on Walter's question. He had no reason to remember September of the previous year. At Auschwitz, all days were the same—slow and painful in the same way—and nobody wanted to remember them. There were no religious or secular celebrations, no holidays, no way of measuring time and its passing except the morning wake-up. It was why the camp inmates came up with their own personal calendars—so they could at least keep track of the seasons and the years, basing them on the most important events in their lives.

Brasse had been at Auschwitz for almost two years now, and his memory of the first year was very confused. He'd been moved from one job to another, constantly needing to learn the rules and obey the orders of a new kommando, and then there had been the fear and ever-present threat of death. These were trials he would rather not remember, and if he had been able to expel them from his mind, he would have done so. The key date for him had been February 15, 1941, the day of his first visit to the Political Department. That date, which he had seen written on a small calendar hanging on the wall behind Walter, was the turning point, the moment when circumstance had handed him the cards he needed to play on an equal footing against his fate.

He remembered lots of things that had happened since then—especially the deaths of his acquaintances from Żywiec and the stoker from Gdańsk—but he could never have managed to place these in a particular month or season. So no, there was no reason why he should remember what happened in September the previous year.

He muttered an embarrassed excuse, and Walter laughed.

"The Russians arrived in September. Don't you remember?"

A light came on in Brasse's mind, and the memory of that time came back to him. A moment before, the Hauptscharführer had seemed to be talking about something in the very distant past, but now everything was so close that along with the memory, the pain returned too. Needles piercing his heart.

"Of course, sir. The Russians."

"There they are! You see how neatly lined up they are?"

The photographer looked. Projected on the wall in front of them were lines of Russian soldiers, worn down by their defeat in battle but still young and strong under the Polish sun. Thousands of them had arrived over the course of a few hours, ready for their first roll call. Not as prisoners of war but as prisoners of Auschwitz.

He remembered how Trałka and Wojcicki had told him of their arrival.

"The Russians are here!" they had laughed. "Finally! Now we'll have some fun!"

His companions in the Erkennungsdienst and he himself hated the Russians with a passion. They had always hated them, even more so when Stalin went into business with Hitler in 1939, allowing him to take Warsaw and even celebrating afterward. Nobody forgot how the "little father" annexed half of Poland without firing a shot. Like any czar or like the imperialists so bitterly criticized by Soviet propaganda.

Predicting a slaughter, Trałka had whispered, "Now they'll get what they deserve."

And indeed, that was precisely what had happened. The SS had reserved seven blocks for the Russians, separating them from the other prisoners only with barbed wire. They had crammed them in there, despite the fact that they couldn't all fit in unless they were huddled one on top of the other. Other than a little bit of soup in the morning, the Germans didn't feed them, didn't look after them, and didn't give them clothes for the increasingly cold weather. They didn't even make them work. They simply kept them there, waiting until they died of hunger. The aim wasn't to exploit them but to exterminate them. Even the Poles in the camp were shocked.

"It's unbelievable," Wojcicki said one day, amazed. "The Germans hate the Russians even more than they hate the Jews."

It was true, and as much as they resented Stalin, Communism, and the Bolsheviks, Brasse and his colleagues could only feel anguish at this spectacle.

"How's it going with the Russians?" Brasse would ask every so often.

"They're dropping like flies," Trałka would answer tersely. Each time he said it, he sounded a little less pleased, and his shoulders drooped a little more.

Only after this first purging phase did the SS put the Russians to work. By then, only a third of them remained, and they, too, were destined to disappear before long. In their physical condition, they couldn't do any work at all, even the lightest tasks. Before the end of November, the seven blocks occupied by the soldiers of the Red Army were once more given over to ordinary Auschwitz deportees, and Russian prisoners were hardly ever seen in the camp again.

As he talked to Walter in the projection room, Brasse found himself remembering a particular day when he had been crossing the camp to deliver a packet of photographs ordered by Dr. Entress, who hadn't sent anyone to collect them. Brasse had passed near the barbed wire around the Russian barracks, and try as he might to keep his eyes lowered, he'd looked up. Curiosity got the better of him, but he wished it hadn't.

On the other side of the wire, he saw ghosts. Spindly, otherworldly beings, standing up, leaning against walls, kneeling on the ground, their arms by their sides, their white skin hanging on their bones, their pale eyes fixed on some distant point. They weren't complaining, weren't asking for anything. To give them a piece of bread would be to hasten their death: they wouldn't even be able to lift a hand to bring it to their mouths.

As he tried to hurry past, Brasse caught one man's eye. He

was right next to the fence, only a meter away. If Brasse had held out his fingers, he would have touched him. He stopped, unable to continue walking.

The man moved his right hand to touch one of the fence poles and opened his mouth. Twice, he tried to speak but failed. He tried once more, and the effort caused two small tears to run down his cheeks. Finally, he spoke a few words in broken German.

"*Ich bin nein Kommunist…*"

Brasse stretched out his arms, powerless. Then he reached through the wire and touched the prisoner's hand. It was as though a tornado had passed through his arm. The man fell backward to the ground, one hand still clutching the fence post. The photographer realized that he was dead.

The Red Army soldier had spoken his last words to him.

Brasse had run away and not looked back.

"Why are you showing me these things, sir?"

In his uneasiness at the memory of the Russian phantom, Brasse turned abruptly to Walter and spoke, but he regretted his words immediately.

Walter had often shown respect for him and his work. They chatted occasionally about technical issues, and the Bavarian was always pleased with Brasse's explanations. Brasse himself judged Walter to be far from the worst of the bosses he could have had. He wasn't evil and didn't beat him or the men in his kommando. He only resorted to shouting and throwing insults in moments of real anger.

Over the course of more than a year, a certain familiarity had grown between the two men, and for the photographer, this was insurance against death, capital to be preserved at any cost. So he immediately repented, having turned to the SS man so impertinently. Never, in any way, should a prisoner behave as though he were on the same level as his boss, no matter how friendly they might be. And sure enough, a shadow of annoyance appeared in Walter's eyes.

"You want to know why I've brought you to the Political Department, don't you, Herr Brasse?"

Brasse nodded without looking up.

"Wait and you'll see. In the meantime, enjoy the film."

Brasse couldn't calm his nerves. He couldn't possibly be there just to watch one of the Hauptscharführer's old films, but only Walter could answer his questions, so he tried to concentrate on the images before him, vivid on the white wall of the room.

The footage now was of a few smiling SS men who saluted the camera as they went around the camp. They were wearing gas masks slung over their shoulders, and Brasse remembered well the terror that had spread among the prisoners at the sight of them. For days, everyone thought that the Germans were preparing to liquidate Auschwitz by dropping bombs on it containing some lethal substance. Anybody who suggested that the gas chambers and the crematoria at Birkenau could do the job of exterminating everyone without the need for bombing was mocked. Soon, all the prisoners were convinced that the apocalypse was near. They were so sure of it and so sure they couldn't escape that they began to work more slowly. It was the resulting beatings from the kapos that proved that the SS did actually want to keep their deportees alive: they wouldn't allow them to loaf about. When nothing happened, the fears of a mass slaughter dissipated but didn't disappear entirely, even when the gas masks disappeared from the SS men's uniforms.

"We had a good laugh at how scared you all were. You were like mice in a cage—terrified but unable to escape. Now, look at this, Herr Brasse."

Men in uniform were sealing up the doors and windows of a building, but it wasn't one at Auschwitz. Skeletal prisoners—Russians on the point of death—were being dragged out of their blocks. Elsewhere, large numbers of sick people were being pulled out of their bunks. There must have been several hundred in total. They were taken to the sealed building and shut inside. None of them protested, none tried to escape: they were too weak to do either. Then, before closing the doors, SS soldiers threw in baskets full of big black tin canisters…

The images faded out, and Brasse was dazzled by the sudden brightness of the wall.

Half a second later, the footage started up again.

It showed the interior of the building. Walter had set up his little film camera against one of the windowpanes.

"I don't want to see, Herr Hauptscharführer!"

Brasse screwed his eyes shut and clutched the arms of his chair.

"If you don't watch, you won't make it to roll call this evening alive."

Seeing that the photographer was keeping his head bowed, Walter repeated his threat in an icy tone. He took his pistol from its holster.

"Do as I say, Brasse, if you want to save your skin."

Brasse obeyed, looking at the wall through his tears.

The prisoners in the building were moving about, anticipating the worst. Disoriented, they scurried here and there, like ants under attack. When the gas began to seep from the black canisters, they moved as far away as they could, piling themselves up against the opposite wall, and then kept swarming from one side of the room to the other, unable to find a way out. The film was silent, its only soundtrack the rumble of the projector, but Brasse could hear the cries of these poor people in his mind. They weren't human screams but the yelps and whines of injured, bleeding animals. The prisoners tried to climb up the walls. They threw themselves against the grating over the windows, trampled over one another, and climbed onto one another's shoulders, but they couldn't escape.

Walter lit a cigarette and offered one to Brasse, who shook his head.

"Take it. It'll help you relax," he encouraged.

With a shaking hand, the photographer accepted reluctantly and put the cigarette between his lips. Walter lit it and watched with amusement as Brasse coughed.

"You're not used to it, are you?"

Brasse didn't answer. He turned back to stare at the wall, hypnotized, letting the cigarette burn out between his fingers. Ash fell onto his uniform, but he didn't notice.

The Russians and the infirm were falling to their knees. A black liquid from their internal organs flowed from their mouths. They lay down on the ground, slowly, as though they were stretching out on their beds at home after a tiring day's work. They were dying unhurriedly, their faces swollen, expiring with a few slight starts. But they were taking too long.

Once in a while, they would lift up their heads, searching for a mouthful of clean air to breathe. Their suffering was inconceivable. It was impossible even to imagine what was going through their minds in those moments.

The film ended, and the reel stopped spooling. The photographer put his head in his hands.

"Send me back to the Identification Service, I beg you."

Walter turned around in the dark and signaled to the projectionist.

Immediately, the lights came on, and the viewing was over. The operator wound the film back, took out the reels, and placed them in a small cardboard box. Then he covered the lens of the projector, saluted, and left the room.

Brasse opened his mouth to speak, but nothing came out. Walter was staring at him, watching his every facial expression for signs of what was going through his mind.

"Have you got anything to ask me?" the officer inquired politely.

Brasse shook his head at first but then raised his eyes to meet the German's gaze.

"I am already your slave, Herr Hauptscharführer. I obey you absolutely. Why did you summon me? Why did you show me that film?"

The SS officer leaned forward and brought his face closer to Brasse's, staring at him.

"You are my slave, Brasse, that's true. But I am not content with your body. I want your mind too. I want to be the master of your conscience, of your soul, of your emotions."

The photographer recoiled. "Why?"

"Because you are one of us. Your father and grandfather are Austrian—*you* are Aryan. And I want you. I want you! Do you remember? I said that to you a year ago when I took you on to work for me."

"I'm Polish…"

Walter's eyes were hard and black.

"Your mother is Polish, and she taught you to believe that you are Polish," he said with scorn. "But what your mother told you doesn't mean anything. What you learned at school and what Piłsudski's propaganda taught you doesn't mean anything. It's blood that matters. And the blood that runs in your veins is largely the same as the blood in mine: Aryan. How long will you persist in denying your people? Is it not time to return to your native land?"

Brasse nodded toward the white wall.

"And what have the Russians and the gas got to do with all that?"

Walter got to his feet and began to pace the room, still scrutinizing Brasse. He answered with another question.

"How long have you been here?"

"Since the thirty-first of August 1940."

"Soon it will be two years. Are you hoping that the war will end?"

"I am sure that it will."

"Are you hoping that Germany will be defeated?"

Brasse didn't answer, and Walter smiled mockingly, shaking his head.

"You must forget about the war, Brasse. Your hopes are senseless. Here we are in Auschwitz—our world ends at the barbed wire. I showed you the film so that you can see we are omnipotent. Your life and death are in our hands. Understand that and you will find it easy to give your heart over to me. I will treat it well. I will give it pride and self-esteem that it has never had before. Come with me, and I will give you the world."

Brasse felt giddy. This man wanted him for his own, but he wasn't trying to buy him or win him over through fear. Walter wanted Brasse to give himself of his own accord. Like a docile, obedient animal. He felt lost and didn't know how to reply.

Walter continued, implacable. "Why, Herr Brasse, do you never leave Block 26? Why do you never leave the Identification Service?"

The photographer looked at him, stunned.

"Do you think I haven't noticed? I know you avoid any external jobs and count on your skill in the studio and photographing the prisoners. But even in there, you're not safe, believe me, and I'm not just referring to physical safety. If I had wanted him to, Kapo Maltz could have killed you long ago. No, I'm referring to your mental state. You think you know who you are and what you want, Brasse, but I'm warning you: if you don't dedicate yourself to me as I want you to, I will drive you to madness."

Brasse looked at him dumbly.

"There's only one way you can save yourself. Give yourself entirely to me, and you won't regret it."

Brasse staggered to his feet and stammered, "Can I go now?"

"Yes, but come back tomorrow morning. I have great plans for you, and I want to tell you about them. Now I'm tired."

Brasse walked out of Block 13 and left the Political Department behind him. He was distraught. He looked up at the sky and saw that night had fallen. For a moment, he was worried that he might have missed roll call before realizing that it was stupid to worry: Walter must certainly have warned Maltz of his absence in advance. Everyone was asleep, but he was too agitated to sleep himself, so instead of returning to his friends in Block 25, he made his way to the Erkennungsdienst in Block 26. He wanted to be alone and was hoping to find it empty.

He was out of luck.

Upon opening the darkroom door, he saw that Myszkowski

was already in there, printing and copying. Whenever Brasse was away from the studio, it was Myszkowski's job to take his place. Brasse walked over to his colleague and tried to concentrate and inspect what Myszkowski was doing. With time, Myszkowski had become very adept, but everything still needed to be checked. As Brasse watched him work, he felt the need to unburden himself.

"Do you remember the Russians, Franek, last autumn?"

The young man stopped tinkering with the enlarger and turned around.

"Of course I do. Why?"

"Do you remember that they died of hunger, and the last ones disappeared at the same time, all of a sudden?"

Myszkowski looked at him curiously. "Yes, I remember... But where've you been? We looked for you all evening and at roll call too, but Maltz answered for you. Did you get into trouble?"

Brasse shook his head, as if to brush off such a foolish question.

"They died, Franek. All those Russians died."

"And so what? All of us will die in here sooner or later."

"Don't you want to know how it happened?"

The boy's lips curled. "Why should I be interested in that? Do you want to tell me all about some new method the Germans have invented for getting rid of prisoners? No thanks, I don't want to know. Let me finish my work. Then I'll finally be able to go to bed. I can barely stand."

Disappointed, Brasse walked away and began fiddling

nervously with the darkroom equipment. Myszkowski finished what he was doing and left.

That night, the photographer slept in the studio, sat with his head resting on the photography desk. He closed the door, but even so, he couldn't shut out the nightmares. The specter of the man from the Red Army held out his hands to him again and again, a question in his eyes.

And Brasse didn't know what to reply.

10

"No more Jews for one thing. There's no point."

"What do you mean, sir?"

"From today, you won't be photographing any more Jews, Brasse. It's completely pointless. Their fate is sealed. They will die. We only waste film and paper by registering them."

Brasse shuddered at the thought of all the Jews who had passed in front of his lens during the busy year he had spent in the Identification Service. He wondered how many there had been. He couldn't come up with an exact number, because the documents with the ever-increasing registration numbers were jealously guarded by the SS, but it seemed an infinite one. Thousands, many thousands—a whole people. With his words, Walter was erasing a whole people from the camp archives. And from history. So easily done it seemed incredible.

Stupidly, Brasse repeated his superior's words. "No more Jews, Herr Hauptscharführer?"

"No. Except for a few special cases that we will pass on to you in due course. The Jews will die, but they are still an excellent object of analysis, and we will be in a better position to study them closely."

"I don't understand, sir."

The SS man smiled. "You don't need to understand now, Brasse. When the time comes, it will all be clear enough. I have great plans for you, as I said. Don't forget that."

The photographer shuddered again.

That morning, he had woken up thinking obsessively about what might await him on his return visit to the Political Department. After having come up with a hundred theories, he had stopped trying to guess. Now he had his first instruction: no more Jews.

Worried by the implications of this, he plucked up his courage and remarked, "No more Jews means far less work. Are you intending to reduce the staff in the Erkennungsdienst, sir? It would be difficult for me to be without one of my colleagues. They are all highly skilled."

The German shook his head. "Don't worry," he replied sarcastically. "Your friends aren't in danger. You'll all stay nice and warm and carry on filling your faces like cats who've got the cream. You'll live because your workload will increase."

The photographer looked at his superior, confused, and waited for an explanation.

"Tell me, Brasse, what do you need to do high-quality retouching?"

So that was it: he was to go back to producing real portraits. Brasse remembered his first summons to the Political Department the previous February and how even then, Walter had asked him endless questions about his retouching skills without explaining why. Did he already have something in mind back then? In any case, Walter didn't know that Brasse already retouched certain photographs of Jewish prisoners—an effective if somewhat hastily done job, carried out using a couple of contraband pens he'd gotten from Myszkowski. He would need far more equipment to serve the German's needs, though.

"To retouch properly, sir, the first thing I need is a new lens."

The SS man was taken aback. "What's wrong with the Zeiss?"

"My Zeiss is excellent but too sharp. It accentuates the face shape and the prisoners' features. It focuses so precisely that even a small bruise becomes an indelible mark. Its lens is more suited to landscapes than portraits, sir. I would need a different one."

"I can't see the link with retouching, Brasse."

The young man tried to explain as simply as possible without seeming arrogant or condescending. Whenever they discussed technical matters, the truth of the matter was clear: Walter was only a talented amateur, and putting him in charge of a whole photography studio hadn't been a very good idea. However, this was certainly not something to point out to the Hauptscharführer.

Brasse was polite and clear. "We need a lens with a softer focus, sir. A proper portrait lens. With that kind of lens, the facial features seem almost out of focus, but they're not, they're just softened. The bruise blends more seamlessly into the skin tone, so less retouching is needed. Do you see?"

Walter listened carefully, and his reaction was enthusiastic. He seemed unaware of the irony hidden in Brasse's question.

"Bravo, Brasse. This is exactly why I chose you! Would another Zeiss do?"

"A Zeiss would be perfect. I'll give you the specifications so you can get the best sort. Also…"

"Also?"

The photographer counted on his fingers the other items he would require.

"As I said last year, I need pencils of specific grades—3H and 4H—and inks, pens, and a brush. And, of course, I need a retouching desk. You know the sort… A table like the ones industrial designers use: sloping and well lit, so you can work at it comfortably. Do you think that's too much, sir?"

"You'll have it all in a few days. I'll send the requisition order to Katowice today, and you'll see, we'll get the very best materials in a flash. Do you want anything else?"

Brasse pondered. This was an opportunity to get something he and his kommando needed. Here was a chance to exploit Walter's offer, but he didn't want to ask for more food or cigarettes. Their standard of living, in Block 26, was already high. He wanted to come up with something more important, something that mattered. Finally, he had an idea.

"If the work is going to increase as you say it will, sir, we might need more staff. Will you authorize me to give you the names of some prisoners with the right skills? If we can find some photographers in the camp, we could use them and be even more productive. What do you think, Herr Hauptscharführer?"

Walter nodded without hesitating. "Granted, Brasse, granted. Tell me who you need, and I'll give them to you, even if they were about to go up in smoke! I'm only a chief squad leader, but we help one another out. And from now on, thanks to you, all my colleagues will owe me something."

"I don't understand, sir."

"You'll understand this evening, Brasse. Now go back to work."

Brasse got to his feet and left the Political Department, praying fervently that he would never have to set foot in there again. He was dazed by these new developments and by all Walter's mysteries. The SS officer was playing with him, like a cat with a mouse, but Brasse was happy that his life hadn't been turned upside down. On the contrary, if his superior was to be believed, he would now be able to dedicate himself even more fully to his work in the Identification Service, closing the door of the Erkennungsdienst on all the terrible things that were happening in Auschwitz.

He was also happy that he'd had the idea of suggesting to Walter that he would need more staff in his kommando: it meant he could save a few lives. It was an extraordinary achievement, and he was so proud of himself that he forgot the threats of the previous evening and Walter's riddles about madness and the great plans in store for him. He went back into Block 26 full of energy, just as the cuckoo was announcing that it was ten o'clock: time to get to work.

He called his colleagues and bent down behind the Zeiss to observe the first subject of the day: a wealthy-looking Romani woman. The Germans seemed to have set to work rounding up Romani living in Europe; this was the third convoy in two weeks. The corridor was full of those who had only just arrived. They were noisy and smelly and were clutching bags that they wouldn't relinquish even in the face of blows and curses. They had come from Bohemia and had the lively faces of people who, after a year of hard work, were about to go on a holiday. They didn't seem to understand where they were, or perhaps they were facing even Auschwitz with the boldness typical of their people.

"They stink! I can't stand them," whispered Trałka in disgust as he prepared the identification sign for the woman lolling in the chair.

Brasse shrugged and smiled. In Żywiec, his hometown, there were very few Romani, but sometimes a group would arrive, set up camp nearby, and stop for a rest. They would walk the streets in pairs—two women, a man with a violin and a child, two children—and try to barter their possessions: copper pots and saucepans, combs, knives, and harmonicas. They didn't ask for handouts, preferring an exchange, and only accepted money when they played their music, livening up the streets, or when the women read girls' palms. They stayed a day, no longer. Then the priests and the police saw them off, and they dismantled their camp, got on their carts, and were off on the road again.

Brasse remembered seeing the caravan of travelers crossing Żywiec to journey up north many times when he was little. Once, he had asked his mother if he could go with them. She had squeezed his hand so hard that it hurt.

"Don't ever say anything like that again, Willy! Those are bad people."

Now the Romani woman was there in front of him, still young, about twenty or twenty-five but already very plump, with an enormous bosom and a large bottom. Out of the corner of his eye, Brasse saw Maltz licking his lips, his expression rapt, and it was clear what he was thinking. The woman took no notice of the kapo, though. Her hair was very dark and uncovered, and she wore a white shirt open at the neck, with a necklace and earrings of imitation jade. Her wide, sloping eyes were dark against her olive skin, and they fixed Brasse, through the lens, with a kind look full of understanding. It was as though she already knew what would happen to her people but was also certain that nothing, not even the Nazis, could uproot the Romani from their soil. The photographer was surprised to realize that never—not once in over a year—had he caught the same look in the eyes of a Jew. Perhaps the Jews had suffered too much in their long history to have any illusions left. Perhaps the Romani were still young enough to have a lot of them to lose. They, too, would eventually give in.

The woman submitted tamely to being photographed, then left. Many others followed—men with hats and mustaches; young, strapping boys; old men bent with age, their skin shriveled; barefoot youngsters; and women with colorful clothes. All those who looked as though they were over thirty—Brasse noticed this detail in particular—had lots of teeth missing or none left at all.

When he began to feel hungry, at about two o'clock, Brasse looked up from the Zeiss and saw Mieczysław Morawa, his friend from the crematorium, enter the studio. He wondered what he could be doing here, but when Morawa gave him a sad, searching look, it was clear that he had come specifically to see the photographer himself. Brasse forgot his hunger, the Romani, and Bernhard Walter. His stomach clenched, and fear entered his heart.

"Let's go in here." He took Morawa into the darkroom. "Has something terrible happened?"

The last time they had met, Morawa had shown him the tattooed skin of the stoker from Gdańsk, an awful thing that had still not stopped the two friends embracing or talking and laughing together. Now there was no time for affectionate gestures. Morawa put his hand in his pocket, pulled out a sheet of paper, and held it out to Brasse, who looked at it and asked, "What is it?"

"It's the presence list from this morning. If they find out I've taken it away, they'll throw me into the furnace alive without even taking my uniform off. Have a look."

The "presence list" was the list of corpses delivered to the crematorium kommando, bodies that Morawa and the others had shoveled up and offered as a sacrifice, a holocaust, to the flames. A long list of names that until the previous day had belonged to living, thinking beings. Nothing remained of them now except a few teeth or bits of bone. Their names, with their hearts and souls, had disappeared into the sky, while the ashes had been collected and would soon fertilize some German colonel's vegetable garden near Auschwitz.

Brasse ran his eyes down the list.

There it was, about the thirtieth line down, at the bottom. So close to salvation, to a day more of life.

His uncle Lech—his mother's brother—was dead. Tears came to his eyes before he could stop them. A sob shook his chest.

"I thought he might be a relative of yours. He was, wasn't he?"

The photographer nodded. Steadying himself against a table, he sat down next to the enlarger. Instinctively, he looked out the window, as if hoping to discover a sign of the final passage from the world of the men listed on that sheet of paper, but the wind had cleared the sky. There were no clouds, and no smoke rose from the chimney. It was all over, all clean, and all that remained of his uncle's life was this name, this fussy bureaucratic entry.

"Did you know him well?"

"He was the one who taught me photography." Brasse smiled at the memory. "He had the best studio in Katowice, and when I was fifteen, he took me on. He gave me my profession. I'm only alive today—" His voice cracked. "Because of him. But what can have happened?"

Morawa shrugged. It was impossible to know.

Brasse couldn't understand. He hadn't had any news of his mother, father, or brothers for almost two years, but he hoped that after his arrest, they'd been careful to keep out of harm's way. He wasn't worried about his parents—they were old now, and he was sure the Germans wouldn't do anything to them. He wasn't even concerned for his three youngest brothers, who were too young to work or be drafted into the Wehrmacht.

The family members he did worry about were his two middle brothers, Bronisław and Jacek, who were two and three years younger than him, the right age for enlisting. The Nazis must have asked them, too, which side they wanted to be on, and there was no way to know how they replied. If they'd refused, he wouldn't be surprised to see them in the studio one of these days, here at Auschwitz, where the most unfortunate Poles ended up.

A day didn't go by when Brasse didn't wonder about their fate, and he would start every time he thought he recognized one of their faces among the deportees. Each day that passed without bad news increased his hope. Perhaps his brothers had gotten away; perhaps they had managed to escape and join the Free Polish Army in England. Perhaps they were safe.

He worried about everyone except for Uncle Lech, who was a calm old man, in love with his work and not at all prone to taking risks. How could he have ended up in a concentration camp? What could he have done to make the Germans seize him from the peace of Katowice and send him to Auschwitz? It was inexplicable.

Brasse smiled bitterly.

"What is it?" Morawa asked.

The photographer waved the piece of paper in the air.

"It's our bizarre destiny that makes me angry. He was on the outside, safe, and being a photographer didn't help to save him. I'm in here, still alive, because I know how to take photographs and print them. Isn't it ridiculous?"

Just then, Franz Maltz poked his head around the door and began to shout furiously.

"Brasse, get out here! Or do I need to drag you out?"

The two friends said goodbye, and finally, Brasse embraced Morawa.

"Thank you for coming over here. And thank you for having taken a risk for me."

"When the time comes, you'll do the same for me." Morawa looked him straight in the eyes, and Brasse realized that his friend was very serious. It wasn't just an empty phrase, he really believed it, and the photographer felt duty-bound to respect this pact.

"I will. When the time comes, I'll do the same. You can count on it."

Dozens of Romani passed in front of his lens that day, with no letup until five o'clock. They were all happy to have their photographs taken, smiling broadly at the Zeiss. Two of them offered sweets to Brasse by way of thanks for his work, but he had to refuse them—he couldn't accept food from deportees while the guards were watching.

Throughout the day, the studio and corridor were filled with the Romani's chatter. Nobody succeeded in silencing them, not even the kapos, common criminals that they were. When the kapos lifted their sticks to beat one of the Romani men or women, the others gathered around with hard faces, shouting insults and taking hold of the kapo's arms or legs until they stopped. If the kapo stepped back to attack from another angle, they crowded around him again, shouting in their incomprehensible language. In the end, they won simply by wearing the kapos down.

After a couple of hours of this, the Romani's kapo disappeared from the corridor, and the studio was left to the Romani. Only Maltz, driven mad by the incessant noise, remained at his post. His job was to stay in the studio, not to accompany the prisoners, and if he'd been found away from his position, he'd have been in trouble. At the end of the day, he, too, breathed a sigh of relief and left immediately.

Then, while Brasse was replacing the protective cover over the lens of the Zeiss, his new subjects appeared at the entrance to the studio in flesh and blood.

11

"MAY WE COME IN?"

Brasse, Trałka, and Brodka looked up and saw three SS men at the door, simple soldiers without any badges or decorations and with the round faces of country boys. There was no need to ask—they were very young, and it was clear that they were on their first assignment, catapulted into the new and fearsome world of Auschwitz from the rural valleys of the Reich. Perhaps from those distant places, even this war seemed glorious. Their faces were so innocent that not even the skulls on their caps instilled any fear. The men of the kommando looked at one another, confused. This was the first time they'd come across SS men who weren't terrifying.

But that wasn't all. One of them cleared his throat.

"I am Schütze Martin Scherr. Hauptscharführer Walter sent me here to get the camp card."

"My name is Frederick Scherr."

"I am Hubert Scherr."

They were brothers, all called to war together, from a Bavarian village not far from Fürth, Bernhard Walter's birthplace. They explained that it had been Walter himself who, during a propagandist recruiting drive, had convinced them to enlist in the SS and follow him to Auschwitz. He had promised the young men booty and prestige.

Brasse felt sorry for them at first, with their innocent eyes, but immediately regretted his sympathy and felt anger rising up inside him. These soldiers were in the same army as the beasts who had murdered his uncle Lech and so many others he had befriended in the camp. It wouldn't be long before they, too, became killers. He kept his feelings to himself, however, and invited them in.

"Welcome. The studio is at your disposal. Which of you is the oldest?"

Martin, the one who had spoken first, stepped forward and sat down in the chair. He had his three pictures taken—full face, profile, and three-quarters with his cap on, like the prisoners. His identification card was the card of a superior, a victor, but in the Erkennungsdienst, the victors got the same treatment as the defeated. Only the uniform was different. And the light in the eyes of the boys. Martin, Frederick, and Hubert looked down the lens with eyes full of nostalgia, and Brasse could see they were thinking of home, of the expressions on their parents' faces when they saw these pictures. They climbed down from the chair like excited children.

"Thank you, Herr Brasse. How can we repay you?"

The photographer brushed off the offer, smiling. "There's no need, sir. This isn't a private studio—we work for Hauptscharführer Walter. Your satisfaction is reward enough for us."

"Now, Herr Brasse, we insist. Do your men not need anything?"

The photographer turned to Brodka and Trałka. He could sense their eagerness to get their hands on something they could use for bartering—food or cigarettes would be ideal—and felt annoyed for a moment, not wanting to compromise himself. Luckily, the Germans solved the problem for him. Martin took a packet of cigarettes out of his pocket and put it on the photography desk. Frederick and Hubert followed suit, and two packets landed on the desk next to the first one.

"Here. One each, from me and my brothers. You can smoke them to our good health."

The three soldiers each shook Brasse's hand and left the studio.

When they were alone, Brasse, Brodka, and Trałka eyed their riches.

"Call the others," Brasse said, and the men in the darkroom— Wojcicki, Wawrzyniak, and Myszkowski—joined the group. "What should we do with them?"

Three packets, with ten cigarettes per packet: thirty cigarettes. In Auschwitz, that was enough to make them rich.

"We'll smoke two packets between us," suggested Myszkowski. "The other one we'll take to the kitchen and exchange for food."

They all agreed with the plan.

"Can you sort out the exchange with the kitchen workers?" Brasse asked, to which Myszkowski gave a nod. "You can all smoke mine," the photographer added. "You know I don't want them."

So the packets were shared between the five smokers in the Identification Service: four cigarettes each. They could enjoy them as though they were free men, as they had been once upon a time, when they could all go into any tobacconist and buy as many cigarettes as they wanted. The packet destined for contraband still lay on the table. Brasse picked it up and weighed it in his hand, almost afraid of spoiling it. Then he put it down again carefully.

"Friends, we've found a gold mine!"

"Please don't move, Herr Unterscharführer."

Brasse leaned over the viewfinder and looked again at the portly SS corporal. His name was Franz Schobeck, and he seemed perfectly suited to the duties assigned to him. When he had come into the studio, Wawrzyniak had nudged Brasse and whispered, "It's the head of the Kanadakommando."

Nobody knew why the kommando had that name or what Canada had to do with it, but everyone in Auschwitz knew what it did: it sorted and redistributed the food and drink confiscated from the deportees at the entrance to Birkenau.

Schobeck, the head of the kommando, wielded enormous power because he got his hands on delicacies that nobody else in Auschwitz ever saw, not even the SS. Rumor had it that all sorts of things ended up on his desk, from bottles of fine French wine to the best cheeses from the pastures of the Baltic. Schobeck was renowned for his large appetite, but not even he could eat everything that came his way, so many of these items became goods for bartering. Nobody could be sure, but it was said that he was partial to precious stones, especially diamonds, and that he was secretly squirreling away an immense fortune.

This explained why Wawrzyniak had nudged Brasse when their new client arrived: it was an invitation to Brasse to exploit the situation. The photographer considered this as he took the photographs.

"Just one more, sir."

He walked over to the corporal and moved his head to the left slightly. Schobeck was about thirty-five and already had the beginnings of an impressive double chin—Brasse needed to make it look as small as possible. He wondered why this man had never risen higher than the rank of corporal. At his age, he could already have become a commissioned officer, especially because the necessities of war made ascending the ranks easier than usual. Brasse tried to find a discreet way of testing the ground.

"You seem in good spirits today, Herr Unterscharführer." He smiled. "Is a promotion in the cards, perhaps?"

The SS man shook his head, frowning. "If only! It seems my superiors prefer to keep me where I am."

"But you have a good reputation here in the camp."

The German looked at him, wondering whether this Polish

man might be making fun of him. But Brasse's face remained completely neutral.

"Yes, I know. I'm respected because I'm good at my job. And luckily, I'm not obsessed with climbing the ladder. For me, wearing the SS uniform is enough. I'm proud of it. It's just a shame I have to keep getting it altered. That's my only problem—food."

Brasse smiled at him, sharing the joke.

"There, all finished. You can get up now."

Schobeck climbed out of the revolving chair with some difficulty. "When can I come and collect the pictures?" he asked.

"In a couple of days, Herr Unterscharführer."

The corporal nodded and left the studio.

Two days later, after the evening roll call, he returned, and Brasse was ready to present him with his identity photographs. Schobeck scrutinized them carefully, checking every detail, even though their small format—six by nine centimeters—made it difficult to see everything clearly. When he looked up, his eyes were shining. He pointed at the three-quarter shot, tapping it with his finger.

"Very good, very good! You've managed to make me slimmer." He put a hand to his neck, patting his double chin with annoyance. "You can't see this so much. And I look younger."

The photographer gave a slight bow, happy that his client was satisfied. Schobeck didn't know it, but this result was thanks to the new Zeiss lens, which had arrived only a few hours before the pictures had been taken. When he'd seen the results, Brasse had been delighted—the lens produced much softer lines in the finished picture, and the photographs no longer looked like rough images from a police identity lineup but real studio portraits. The chubby corporal had been the first to benefit, and Brasse was determined to get something out of it.

"I am always at your disposal, for any kind of work."

Schobeck took the hint. He looked over his shoulder to check that Walter wasn't in sight. The chief squad leader had accompanied him to the Identification Service, stopping to chat for a while and leaving only a few moments earlier. Now that his superior had gone, the corporal unbuttoned the jacket of his uniform and withdrew a dark-colored envelope, which he handed to Brasse.

"Look at these pictures."

Brasse opened the envelope and took out two old, battered black-and-white photographs with white, scalloped edges. He bit his lip, foreseeing difficulties, but he couldn't let the chance pass him by.

"Let me guess. Are these your parents, sir?"

Schobeck nodded, buttoning up his jacket again. He pointed to the photograph in Brasse's left hand.

"Yes, this one is my parents. The other one is my grandparents—my father's parents."

"What would you like, exactly?"

"I'd like you to enlarge them. Can you make them double the size?"

The photographer didn't reply straightaway. He scratched his chin thoughtfully.

"They're not in good condition. They're crumpled and a bit stained. And you see those lines? It won't be easy to get rid of them. They're also faded. The black and white have turned an ugly gray, and that would need to be corrected. A tricky job…"

The corporal took him by the elbow in a friendly way.

"Is it a problem that we might be able to resolve, one way or another?"

Brasse felt his excitement growing. He had to decide. If he was mistaken in his assessment of the man standing next to him, he'd be taken out to the wall behind Block 11 and have a bullet put in his head for trying to corrupt an SS man. He hoped that all the experience he'd gained at Auschwitz in observing human vices would stand him in good stead. He decided to take the risk.

"It could be done, but…"

"But?"

Brasse looked him in the eye and said in a lighthearted tone, "I'd need a loaf of bread for the developing and fixing, and I'd need a block of margarine for my work. A whole block of margarine."

He smiled, and Schobeck returned the smile. But the corporal had understood, and his reply couldn't have been more serious.

"You'll have everything you want, Herr Brasse. Come to the bakery tomorrow, and I'll give you all of it. But make sure you do a good job for me."

The German left, and Brasse sat down and took a deep breath.

He was frightened by his own recklessness and asked himself

a hundred times how he could have been so imprudent. He had never thought himself capable of taking such risks. Then he looked up and saw the whole kommando gathered around him. They didn't say anything, but they knew what had happened. Alfred Wojcicki put a hand on his colleague's shoulder, a silent question in his eyes.

"Bread and margarine," Brasse replied. "Tomorrow morning."

The others hugged one another in delight.

Straight after roll call the next morning, Brasse went to the bakery near the kitchen block, where he had worked for a while, not long after his arrival at Auschwitz. He was met by Schobeck himself, who, without saying a word, passed him a long loaf of black bread and a huge block of margarine. When the SS man had turned away, another prisoner beckoned to Brasse and handed him a bucket. Inside was enough margarine to last days and days. The photographer ran away with his treasure, rushing along the path to Block 26, jumping every time he met anyone.

Back at the Erkennungsdienst, everything was divided among the kommando except for a small share destined to be bartered for other goods.

"We've got to make sure to please the Unterscharführer now."

That very evening, Brasse got to work. He used the new lens to photograph the prints that Schobeck had given him, hoping to make the imperfections of the originals less obvious. From these negatives, he printed new, larger pictures of the corporal's parents and grandparents. Wanting to curry favor, he made the prints even larger than requested—now Schobeck would be able to frame them to impressive effect. He also corrected the contrast and brought the black and white tones back to their original splendor.

All that remained was the retouching work, and for this, he enlisted the help of Wawrzyniak, who was not only a good calligrapher but also a skilled artist. Brasse asked him to strengthen the outlines of the figures and their facial features, to create a more painterly effect. Brasse only intervened later to darken areas that were too light, using soot, which he then fixed with varnish. Finally, the pair admired their handiwork. Schobeck's parents seemed to be alive. It was as though the picture had been taken that very day at the Identification Service. No professional could have done a better job.

When Schobeck came to collect the photographs, he took them and laid them on a table. He looked at them carefully and reached out his hands as though to touch his relatives' faces. Then he drew back, not wanting to spoil the portraits. He sighed, sat down, and turned to Brasse.

His voice trembled. "They're beautiful! Thank you, thank you!"

The photographer smiled. "Our mothers and fathers, Herr Unterscharführer, are the dearest people of all to us. I wanted to honor the memory of yours, just as I would have done for my own."

Schobeck couldn't take his eyes off the images. Before leaving, amid a torrent of thanks, he said to Brasse, emphasizing every word, "Come and see me whenever you want to, Brasse. You'll always find something to eat!"

Brasse lowered his head and didn't reply, but after that, he went to the bakery two or three afternoons every week, and Schobeck gave him bread and margarine every time. Not only that, but when Schobeck's back was turned, the men from the bakery kommando would add something else to his bag.

Brasse was happy. He was now able to give his colleagues food, and not only them. One afternoon, he returned from the bakery to find two acquaintances from Katowice waiting for him—two boys who'd been at school with him. They held out their hands and asked for bread. Then the two became three, then four and five, until finally there were around a dozen men waiting for him. Brasse gave them all bread and margarine twice a week.

None of his Identification Service colleagues protested about all this generosity. It was their duty to share, and that meant sharing with beggars. They had the right to eat too.

This plenty lasted for three months until one day, Brasse bumped into Schobeck a long way from the bakery and the kitchens. The SS man stopped, looked him in the eye, and spoke to him in a falsely friendly tone.

"Brasse, I know you steal. But until I catch you at it, there's nothing I can do about it."

The photographer froze. The warning couldn't be clearer. He clutched his cap in his hands and murmured an apology as the corporal pushed past him.

From that day on, he stopped going to the bakery and bothering the head of the Kanadakommando, but the supply of provisions from elsewhere didn't dry up. In fact, the SS came knocking more and more often at the door of Block 26. They didn't just want to have their identification cards done. Often they wanted real portraits, which then needed to be printed in postcard format to send to wives, mothers, and brothers. They also brought all sorts of family photographs: themselves with their parents, playing in the fields when they were young, or paddling in the river with friends. They wanted enlargements, copies, or close-up prints of particular details.

They came with Walter's permission, which meant they didn't have to go to a studio in town and also built up the credit that Walter had mentioned to Brasse. They were also very generous, especially when there were women involved in their requests. They would have their picture taken for a girl back in Germany or request an enlargement of a picture of her, and they were happy to pay for them.

Although the soldiers were in no way obliged to compensate Brasse and his kommando, they wanted to, and so it was that as well as margarine and cigarettes, the studio began to fill up with cheese, sausages, and cookies. The cupboard in the darkroom was never empty now, and Brasse himself got better at asking for things. It only needed a nod or a wink, and the SS men understood that the Identification Service would like to be paid with something tangible. It was a courage that was easy to acquire: just a look, no words.

The first time had been difficult, but then it came naturally. Corporals, sergeants, captains, and lieutenants all gave freely. Only when faced with the most hostile, unpleasant characters did Brasse keep his eyes lowered and play the role of the obsequious servant. He followed his instinct about when to stay quiet. In this way, life in the Erkennungsdienst improved very pleasingly, and the kommando couldn't complain about how things were going.

13

THIS STATE OF AFFAIRS WAS DEALT WITH SIMPLY AND brutally but not without ceremony.

The square was full for roll call. When the count had been done, the SS ordered the men to remain where they were. The reason for this soon became clear.

The deputy commandant of the camp appeared on the small stage that had been set up for special occasions. Brasse was in the second row and was able to observe him at close quarters for the first time. He had only seen him once before—on August 31, 1940, the day he had arrived in Auschwitz on a cattle car—but he had never forgotten this man's face or his voice.

His face was slim, with tight lips and thin cheeks, and his forehead was so large that it seemed out of proportion to the rest of his face. He had blond hair, and his blue eyes were constantly moving, full of disdain. His voice was like his gaze: it betrayed neither concern nor pity for the prisoners, only a desire to complete his tasks as quickly as possible.

On that late August evening back in 1940, the deputy commandant had spoken only for about a minute, addressing the convoy that had arrived from Tarnów.

"Men, this is not a sanatorium. This is a concentration camp. Here, a Jew lives for two weeks, a priest for three weeks. An ordinary prisoner might live three months. But all must die. Remember that! If you remember it, you will suffer less!"

Those words rushed back into Brasse's mind. More than two years had passed since then, and he had seen this prophecy borne out. No trace remained of the thousands of Jews who had passed in front of the Zeiss at the Erkennungsdienst. He had forgotten all about the priests. Of the prisoners who had arrived with him from Tarnów, very few were still alive. He, Brasse, was one of that small number.

He breathed deeply, afraid again.

Over the last few months, he had felt calmer and had stopped fearing the outside world of the camp quite so much. He was the camp photographer, and that made him untouchable. He might be a cog in the Auschwitz machine, but he wasn't the least important or the most defenseless cog. He was no longer terrified of being beaten up from one moment to the next. The long period he had spent in Block 26 had gradually made him feel more secure. He did, however, occasionally feel a new emotion, one that he didn't want to admit to feeling, even to himself: guilt.

This emotion came precisely from this increased sense of well-being. He was alive. He was an "ordinary prisoner," but he had gone far beyond the three months' survival predicted by the deputy commandant. He had managed it on his own merits, but this didn't reduce his unease. He knew he had stooped to making a pact with the Germans—the assassins, the criminal beasts who any man worthy of the name wouldn't go anywhere near. And he accepted their gifts. He hadn't yet given himself fully to them, as Walter desired, but he knew he had set off along a dangerous path.

These unpleasant thoughts assailed him every so often—when he was in the darkroom in the evening, or at night when he was lying on his bunk staring at the ceiling—and he would chase them away. Now, as he stood motionless in the crowd at roll call, they took hold in his mind, and he couldn't quell them. He was growing increasingly nervous, and to calm himself down, he focused on the deputy commandant.

The SS man looked at the throng of prisoners for a moment. He took off his cap, handed it to a subordinate, and ran a hand through his hair. Then he put his mouth to the microphone. Again, his speech was extremely short. It seemed he was not one to waste his breath.

"You deportees have only one rule: to obey the rules of the camp. Whoever breaks the rules of the camp will be punished, and whoever commits the most serious offenses will be punished

by death. This is why you are here listening to me: because I, your
superior, want to reaffirm the Auschwitz law. And I want you to
remember it. Let none of you get any more strange ideas into your
heads. Only those who submit to the whip will survive. Whoever
rebels will die. Is that clear?"

The men in the square chorused a loud "Yes!" Now they
understood: they had been called to witness an execution. All eyes
turned to the gallows. Two nooses were hanging from a heavy
horizontal beam resting on two vertical beams; the final stage
for condemned prisoners was a bleak, abject gibbet. A man and
a woman appeared in a corner of the square and were pushed
toward the gallows by their kapos. They struggled and thrashed,
gasping through clenched teeth, but didn't emit a sound. Held by
three men each, they were forced to climb up onto a chair, and
their heads were placed in the nooses. When they stood up, Brasse
recognized the man.

He grabbed the arm of Stanisław Tralka, who was standing
next to him.

"I know him!"

Tralka looked at his friend in astonishment. "Is he from your
town?"

"No, but before I started at the Identification Service, we
used to sleep in the same barracks. His name's Galiński—Edward
Galiński. He's only a boy. What did he do?"

Tralka shrugged. "He escaped with his woman, but they got
him. She went into a shop near the Slovakian border to buy food,

and they caught her. When he saw her with a policeman, he came out of his hiding place because he didn't want to abandon her. That's what I've heard."

Brasse studied Galiński's face. It was swollen from the blows he'd received during his interrogation, but even now, as he was being slaughtered, it still carried a smile. The young man looked to his left: he was smiling at the girl. She, too, had been beaten. Her hair was wild, her uniform torn, and the bruises on her arms and legs made her seem ugly and old, but her beloved saw something quite different. And with this image in his eyes, Galiński was put to death.

The SS kicked the chairs out from underneath them, and their bodies dangled in the air, a foot and a half from the ground.

They writhed for less than a minute. She was the first to die. He followed immediately afterward.

During the execution, the kapos kept an eye on the prisoners in the square and brutally beat any who dared to avert their eyes from the spectacle.

Death, if it was to fulfill its instructive purpose, had to be public.

Everyone had to watch and learn, in silence.

Brasse had understood this lesson a long time ago, and it was of no use to him. When he recognized Galiński, his fear increased, and he hoped that they would soon be sent back to their barracks. He didn't want to stay out in the open a moment longer than was necessary.

The photography studio and the darkroom were the only bearable realities to him. Outside the Identification Service, madness was taking hold—real madness, not the kind that Walter displayed with his boasting threats. Brasse experienced the same feeling of inadequacy as he had at the crematorium the day Morawa had shown him the stoker's tattooed skin ready to be tanned. He wasn't ready to accept it all.

He prayed to God to take him back to his refuge, and when he was finally there, shut away inside Block 26, he asked forgiveness of his friend who had been hanged. As he sat there, he wondered which was the more courageous act: to risk hanging by running away from the camp or to get in with the SS as he had done and receive an extra piece of bread each day for himself and his companions.

Sleep overcame him before he could find an answer.

14

BRASSE BENT DOWN AND PICKED UP THE POSTCARD
from the floor.

He had just seen the last deportee of the afternoon leave the
Erkennungsdienst, and his eye had fallen on a black-and-white
picture that had been dropped in the corridor.

It was of a sea view—a coastline with clear water, a perfectly
white beach and lush vegetation in the background, with a few
white houses here and there. The title printed on the back read
Near Calvi, Corsica, but what attracted Brasse's attention was a
short, almost illegible handwritten phrase, scribbled down hastily
in French: "From Jean to his brother, tell him that..."

Thanks to his basic grasp of the language, which he had
picked up in the camp, Brasse deciphered the meaning of the

words and saw that the message was incomplete. The phrase ended with a scrawl, as though the pen had been seized from the hand of the man trying to leave a hurried final testimony for his family. This must have happened while Brasse had been photographing the prisoners several feet away in the studio. The owner of the postcard must have passed in front of the Zeiss, and who could say how he'd thought he might get this little piece of printed card out of the camp.

Brasse looked again at the picture and felt a rush of immense regret for everything he could have done if he hadn't been imprisoned in Auschwitz. He'd never seen the sea, except at the cinema, had never smelled it or seen the blue of the waves. He'd never felt its breeze on his face. People had told him about it— Uncle Lech, for example, who had visited Western Europe and the Mediterranean after his marriage and described it as an enchanted place where people were always happy and ate wonderful food. But that was all, and Brasse didn't know if he would ever see it in this lifetime. In any case, not even the magic of the Mediterranean sun had saved the Corsicans from deportation. A convoy of them had arrived just the evening before, and he'd spent the day photographing them.

At that moment, the door of Block 26 opened, and Walter entered the building with a higher-ranking officer. Even if Brasse hadn't noticed the man's epaulets, he would have identified the difference in rank just from Walter's behavior. He was actually bowing down to his superior. As Brasse took another look at the new arrival, he saw with a shudder that it was Maximilian Grabner, the head of the Political Department. He'd caught sight of this man around the camp several times—Grabner was always surrounded by a gaggle of subservient admirers—but he'd never spoken to him.

The two SS men made their way over to Brasse, and Walter said meaningfully, "Herr Brasse, may I introduce Untersturmführer Grabner, our manager."

The photographer dropped the postcard and stood to attention, removing his cap.

"Prisoner 3444! Present!"

Brasse glanced anxiously at the three silver pips on Grabner's collar; it was the first time he'd been near such a high-ranking SS man. As head of the Political Department, Grabner was not only Walter's superior but also the boss of the whole Identification Service, the head of the kommando. And he had a grim reputation, especially among the Poles, because his main task had been to eliminate the intelligentsia of that country since its invasion in 1939. On a regular basis, he repeated this information to his subordinates, who were careful to spread the word, terrifying the deportees.

There were endless rumors of Grabner's pitilessness, his cynicism, and his indifference to all those around him—friends included. Brasse had never actually heard that Grabner murdered prisoners himself—that was a lowly task left to his underlings— but nevertheless, having this man in front of him made him feel naked and defenseless.

"Hauptscharführer Walter has told me about you, Herr Brasse, and I wanted to take the chance to visit the Erkennungsdienst. I'm in charge of it, and I should have come sooner, but I have so many responsibilities."

"Of course, sir. Would you like me to show you around?"

Grabner nodded his assent.

As they passed into the studio, Brasse glimpsed Walter gesturing wildly at him, a nasty look in his eye. "Make a good impression," those gestures meant, "or you're in for it." The photographer nodded calmly and led Grabner to the desk with the Zeiss and then into the darkroom, explaining in detail how he worked and what the team did.

The rest of the kommando was there, and as soon as they saw the SS man, they scrambled to line up in front of him, but he told them not to stand at attention.

"Concentrate on your work, and don't take any notice of me."

It was impossible, though, not to think about him and the power he wielded. There was always the possibility that he had sentenced one or all of them to death before coming to Block 26, and he was here to amuse himself, to survey his realm before exterminating the people. Brasse felt the tension among the men rising with each second that passed and sensed every eye fixed on their backs. Even Walter couldn't contain himself any longer.

"Herr Untersturmführer, our head photographer is a real artist, as I told you. Would you not like to take the opportunity to have your portrait taken?"

Grabner turned around and noticed all the men staring at him. He gave a brief, scornful smile and shrugged his shoulders carelessly.

"Why not? I haven't had my photograph taken since my last day in Paris. What do I need to do?"

At this, Brasse saw Walter turn pale and begin to tremble. His superior usually gave orders rather than asking for them. Walter opened his mouth to speak, but nothing came out. He looked pleadingly at the photographer, begging him to step in.

Brasse took a deep breath. After all, this man was just another "client" in his studio, and he should treat him as such. Just like in the old times in the shop in Katowice, with Uncle Lech.

"Come this way, sir." He smiled pleasantly and pointed to the revolving chair.

Everyone watched Grabner sit down in the chair that had accommodated the posteriors of Jews, Romani, criminals, and outcasts from half of Europe and held their breath, hoping for a moment like in fairy tales, when a spell might transform their persecutor into a pig. But nothing happened. Grabner was still Grabner: small, wiry, white, and Aryan.

He looked at Brasse with satisfaction.

"A very comfortable chair," he declared. "I'm ready!"

The photographer shook himself and looked through the viewfinder.

The SS second lieutenant gazed at the lens with a relaxed expression, and his eyes lost their usual unpleasant sharpness;

now they were peaceful, almost laughing. He looked like a human being, and Brasse suddenly found himself wanting to make a really good portrait of this man.

Yes, he thought with a rush of professional pride. This was his chief, and he wanted to please him.

"Have you got a comb, sir?" he asked, getting up from the desk.

Grabner, surprised, felt in the pocket of his trousers. "Yes, I do."

"Could you comb your hair, please?"

Grabner tidied himself up as requested, pulling back his thinning hair with rapid movements. Brasse, meanwhile, arranged the lights at the correct distance from the chair. He'd quickly sized up his subject and decided that this face needed delicate shadows: the features needed to seem soft. Grabner was around forty, and Brasse hoped that the Zeiss lens might make him seem younger, fresher.

"Now smile slightly, Herr Untersturmführer."

Grabner attempted a smile, but it quickly disappeared. His eyes became cold again, and his features hardened, as though the thought of the work piling up in the Political Department had suddenly flashed into his mind.

He realized this. "I'm sorry. I'll try again."

Brasse held up his hands. "It doesn't matter, sir. Tell me, where are you from?"

Grabner raised his eyebrows. "What's that?"

"Which part of Germany are you from, sir?"

Nobody ever talked to Grabner so informally, and Brasse heard Walter, who was leaning against the wall close by, give a sharp intake of breath.

"From a village in the Black Forest."

"Very well, sir—think about your village. Think of the woods and the beautiful place where you lived when you were young."

Grabner closed his eyes for a moment, and his face relaxed.

"Now look at the camera, please."

The SS man turned obediently toward the lens and opened his eyes. Brasse pressed the shutter release button.

"Done! We have a perfect portrait," he declared with a mixture of anxiety, conviction, and fear.

Only then did the men of the kommando allow themselves to breathe. Life, which had been suspended for a long minute, began again.

"We can go now, Untersturmführer, if you wish," Walter ventured.

But Grabner took no notice of his subordinate. He stood up and began to examine the studio once again, very slowly, and then went into the darkroom. He scrutinized the equipment silently and carefully, looking over the prisoners' shoulders as they worked. This time, nobody accompanied him. Everyone observed his strange behavior in silence and waited for him to tell them what he wanted.

Finally, he turned to Brasse.

"Tell me, Herr Brasse, what do your men say about me?"

"Excuse me, sir?"

Grabner looked at him coldly.

"You understood me perfectly well. What does your kommando say about me?"

The photographer cleared his throat, thinking quickly. "That you are an excellent chief, sir. That we couldn't have a better one. And that Hauptscharführer Walter is an excellent manager of the Identification Service."

"That's enough. Don't overdo the flattery... You're afraid, aren't you?"

Brasse didn't reply, and Grabner shook his head, smiling.

"You know I have never killed anyone?"

The photographer trembled, wondering what this fiend was up to.

"I know, sir."

Grabner opened his arms wide. "I could do it. We are at war. There is nothing more normal in times of war than killing one's enemies. And who are Germany's enemies, Herr Brasse?"

Brasse again said nothing. He didn't know how to reply. Whatever he said would be wrong.

"Germany's enemies are the animals shut in the bunker."

Brasse turned pale, still standing to attention.

Only two minutes earlier, he had been giving this man instructions as though they were in any peacetime studio. Now the SS man was reasserting the power he wielded over them all. The hunter instinct had returned. Brasse didn't know what happened to the prisoners in the bunker—those being punished for misdemeanors—and he certainly didn't want to find out. But Grabner was determined to explain it to him, to make him party to this personal secret. The photographer felt the urge to cover his ears, but he couldn't. Walter, meanwhile, was trembling like a leaf. Grabner began to speak again, leaning close to Brasse, looking him in the face, but he raised his voice so the whole kommando could hear.

"I want you to share this little duty with me. Once a week, I have the list of prisoners locked in the bunker brought to me, usually on a Saturday. I call them before me one by one. Lachmann, my assistant, is a good SS man and studied in your schools: he speaks Polish and translates for me. I ask each one his name, how he came to be in the camp, and what work he does. For me, these prisoners are not numbers but God's creatures, and I must take an interest in them. That is why I ask so many questions.

"Then I ask each one why he has been punished. Unfortunately, their 'sins' are always the same. It's extremely boring. One has been punished because he didn't finish his work, another because he didn't get up in the morning. I look carefully at their faces, searching for a flicker of divine light in their eyes. After all, the same being who gave me life gave them life. But I am always disappointed. I find them to be beasts. I see before me terrified animals in chains. Tell me, Brasse, what greatness is there to be found in a man who gives in at the first difficulty?"

The photographer didn't reply, and Grabner's question was

met with total silence. Nobody moved or breathed. Walter had hidden behind the revolving chair.

"No greatness," the officer supplied. "If I saw a little pride in their eyes, I would save them. I would even send them home. But when they stand in front of my desk, they have already lost the battle. They have turned their backs on God, and God has abandoned them. Believe me, by then, it makes no difference whether they live or die. I choose. After the interrogation, I put an *O* or an *X* next to each name. Those marked *O* are lucky: they are assigned to the penal company. There, they perform hard labor and, if they are strong enough, can gain redemption. Those marked *X* are also fortunate, in their own way. My men take them to the wall of Block 11. You know what happens by the wall of Block 11, don't you?"

This time, Brasse did reply. "Yes, sir. We all know."

Grabner brought his face even closer to Brasse's and put a hand on his shoulder.

"Is what we are doing right, Brasse?"

The photographer looked at Grabner with tears in his eyes. He shrugged his shoulders, defeated, and looked at the floor.

The Untersturmführer sighed, shook himself, and flicked an invisible speck of dust from his jacket.

"My superiors always tell me that history will be the judge. That is stupid, and I'm not a child who simply repeats the teacher's lessons. I am not waiting for history. I know that you and your men have judged me, Brasse. Well? What is your sentence?"

Brasse did not have the courage to raise his eyes, and all the men in the kommando looked away.

Grabner waited in vain for a reply.

He banged a fist on the table in disappointment and gestured impatiently at Walter.

"Let's go, Herr Hauptscharführer. I was curious to meet them, but even these are not men. They are only afraid—they are animals too. They don't interest me. Let's be on our way." Then, before he reached the door, he turned back once more. "Hauptscharführer Walter defends you and tells me you're indispensable, but there's plenty of room in the bunker, and I'm tempted to add a good few from this kommando. Be careful."

And he left the room, with Walter at his heels.

The men of the Erkennungsdienst sat down, breathless.

As a student, Alfred Wojcicki knew he was doomed to be one of Grabner's victims: "student" meant "intelligentsia," and sooner or later, the head of the Political Department would have him eliminated. The boy broke down in tears.

The others didn't say another word for the rest of the day.

After roll call that evening, Brasse returned to the studio to develop and print the portrait of Grabner. When it was done, he took a careful look at it. He really had done a good job, especially in finding the right balance of light and shade, but what struck him most was the expression in the man's eyes. The gaze was open and serene, just as it had seemed through the viewfinder. Brasse hadn't been mistaken—he had found a trace of humanity there. Then he remembered Grabner's words and felt ashamed of his momentary empathy. Briefly, his heart had forged a link between him and his oppressor.

He let the picture fall to the ground as if it had burned his fingers and left the room.

That night, Untersturmführer Grabner slept smilingly on the floor of Block 26.

15

"THIS IS A DAY OF CELEBRATION FOR US ALL. IT SEEMS strange, here in the camp, but it's true. Today, we're happy, and we can even forget our suffering. Today, there is no place for pain or foreboding. There's only joy on this special evening. You know me, and you can guess why I wanted to say a few words. I couldn't hope for a better occasion to thank my dear friend Rudolf…"

The speaker's voice cracked with emotion, but everyone applauded, encouraging him to continue. He was a man of advancing years with unmistakably Slavic features who expressed himself in faltering Polish. His name was Juri Sebianski. His intelligent eyes shone in a face crisscrossed with wrinkles. His open expression gave him a trustworthy look, and it was true that his fellow prisoners did have faith in him. After a short pause, he managed to continue.

"As you know, I am a school teacher. I taught history and geography in Minsk for a very long time, and far more students than I can remember passed through my classroom over the years. Unfortunately, and you know this too, teachers have no place in Auschwitz. Our captors already know everything and have no need for lessons. They hate teachers. As for my fellow prisoners... I couldn't teach those I share a bunk with anything about how to survive. Things can't be taught. They are simply learned. I should have ended up shoveling gravel in a quarry or on a construction site or carrying bricks all day. That would have been the end of me. But instead, I'm alive..."

His voice became a whisper, and tears appeared in his eyes. This time, there was no applause, and his audience waited silently for him to go on. Sebianski swallowed his sobs and looked up to meet the eyes of Rudolf Friemel, who was standing next to him. He put his hand on Friemel's shoulder and gave it a squeeze.

"I'm alive thanks to you, my dear Rudolf. You took me and turned me into an artisan. Never in all my life would I have thought I'd become an expert at making stoves. But that's what happened: today, my hands create beautiful ceramic tiles for stoves. That shows two things. First, that humans are infinitely resourceful: they can get over any difficulty if they want. Second, not all kapos are bad. You are a good kapo, the very best kapo. So long live Rudolf and Margarita! Long live the bride and groom!"

Sebianski's final words were met with a thunderous round of applause and shouts of approval. It was true: not every kapo was a brute. The destiny of the deportees was not already decided, and there still existed a world outside Auschwitz. On occasions such as this, it was even possible to imagine that the camp would only be a phase in their lives. One day, perhaps, they would relegate it to the most hidden parts of their memory, trying to forget it, and they might even stop asking themselves why it had happened. As though reading one another's thoughts, Brasse, Trałka, and Myszkowski exchanged glances, laughing and nudging one another.

"It would be wonderful to make it through, wouldn't it?" mused Trałka.

Brasse shook his head. "Hoping to make it through is the best way to be made a fool of."

"But we endure. We eat and sleep together, work together. Not even the SS and the kapos have gotten rid of us. Why shouldn't I hope?"

Brasse shrugged. "You don't need me to tell you that, Stanisław. You've seen enough to know that our lives are in their hands. Always, in every way. Walter snaps his fingers, and we go up in smoke. I live from day to day, hour to hour. Now be quiet. I want to hear what Rudolf has to say."

Rudolf Friemel got to his feet, and everyone fell silent.

He tapped his glass with a fork to create the right atmosphere and smiled. He looked very elegant; civilian clothes suited him well. He was wearing a black pinstripe suit, an immaculate white shirt, and a bright red-and-blue tie that his parents had bought for him in Vienna. Next to him, just as elegant, sat Margarita Ferrer, the young Spanish woman whom Friemel had married barely an hour earlier in the camp registry office.

Wilhelm Brasse had been their witness and had been granted permission to wear civilian clothes for the first time since his arrival at Auschwitz. His outfit was nothing special—a jacket, pair of trousers, shirt, and hat thrown together from belongings taken from deportees who'd arrived the previous day—but taking off the striped uniform had been a disturbing experience.

It felt strange to touch his chest, almost unconsciously, and no longer feel the triangle that informed the world of his status as a prisoner. He could escape, wearing these clothes. It was a passing thought; the guards took them away from him right after the ceremony and made him put the camp uniform back on. Such a rapid transformation highlighted his sense of oppression. It was as though he had tasted liberty but for too short a time.

The deputy commandant had attended the wedding, and Brasse couldn't help but notice that he always seemed equally at ease in his role as executioner and as the smartly dressed officer attending his friends' wedding. Bernhard Walter had attended on behalf of the Political Department, and the ceremony had been conducted under the watchful gaze of soldiers bearing rifles.

Rudolf and Margarita had sealed their vows of love and fidelity with the exchange of rings.

"I will love and cherish you always," the groom had said, his voice full of emotion.

"I will love and cherish you always," Margarita had replied simply.

All those present knew that Rudolf and Margarita would keep their promises, because nothing could stand in the way of a love solemnized at Auschwitz.

Rudolf's parents, the prisoners, and the SS had all applauded, urging the two young people to kiss. They had exchanged just one long, passionate embrace.

Now everyone was in Block 26, where the Erkennungsdienst had obtained permission from the Germans to organize a small party. Rudolf was well known throughout the camp because he had helped so many deportees to survive, and it had been easy to put together a fine buffet. No block had been unwilling to donate. There were embroidered tablecloths, china plates, glasses and crystal champagne flutes, linen napkins, place cards, and the best of Austrian cuisine in honor of Friemel's origins.

Everything had sprung miraculously from within Auschwitz. And everyone was enjoying themselves. The groom's speech was interrupted several times by gales of laughter. He could speak relatively freely: the SS had been considerate enough to make themselves scarce, and he made the most of their absence to make a few jokes.

"I thank you all and should warn you that it's no use asking Margarita to make a speech—she's a strong woman, but she's shy and not used to an audience like this. And there isn't much I want to say. We got married today, but we've known and loved each other for six years, since the Spanish Civil War. Don't worry. I'm the criminal. I'm the Communist, the Red Aryan, the one who sold himself, as our dear Führer would say, to the international Demo-Pluto-Judaic cause. She doesn't get involved in politics, and she's right not to. She's free, while I am imprisoned in Auschwitz.

"But I don't want to think about those things now. I want to say something much more important. Margarita and I love each other, and we always will. But if something should happen to me…" Friemel's tone suddenly turned serious. "I entrust her and our child to each one of you, to be looked after. He must survive. I want him, at least, to live in a world of peace and liberty, and if I can't fight for that, I want you to fight for me. Promise! Promise with your hearts."

He sat down, overcome with emotion, and held his wife's hand tightly while the child, a chubby toddler with black curly hair like his father's, crawled around among the guests. They all lifted their glasses, and Brasse smiled at Rudolf's parents, taking the chance to observe them.

They were quite old, respectable bourgeois people, who had made a request to Himmler in person for their son, a German citizen, to be allowed to get married in the camp. They had waited patiently and stubbornly for several months for permission to be granted. In the end, they had come all the way to Auschwitz to be present at the ceremony and had suddenly been plunged into a world beyond the conception of any normal person. They had seen the barracks, the kapos, the prisoners, the SS. They had heard the cries and seen that people here suffered in a way that no words could possibly describe. Their fear and disorientation showed on their faces. They were clearly happy to be at their son's wedding but more fearful for him than ever.

The bare, ugly reality was too much for them.

Brasse had been feeling joyful until that point but now fell back into sadness. There were such insurmountable obstacles between Rudolf's little son, Edi, and a future of peace and liberty, starting with the barbed wire that divided Rudolf and the other prisoners at Auschwitz from the world outside.

They all knew Friemel's story. He was a Viennese Communist who had volunteered in the Spanish Civil War. After Franco had conquered Madrid, Friemel had found himself with no homeland, as Hitler had invaded Austria in the intervening period. He had fled to France with Margarita. But history did not stop pursuing Rudolf. The Germans then occupied Paris, and they sent Rudolf back to Vienna and then to Auschwitz, where they intended to make him pay for his political crimes.

Friemel, however, was too clever even for the Nazis. He was an expert in repairing diesel motors, and this skill had allowed him to rise up through the ranks of the camp hierarchy, eventually becoming an oberkapo and one of the most important workers in Auschwitz. He was allowed many liberties: he could grow his hair, he ate the same meals as the SS, and once a week, he was allowed to go to the cinema in Oświęcim, accompanied by a soldier.

Rudolf had immediately begun to use his own privileges for

the benefit of others, and he quickly became a legend among the prisoners. He always knew where to place those who were most in need; you only had to ask, and you could be sure that he would find the right kommando for someone who was weak, ill, or old. They would have a job that allowed them to survive. Brasse had known him from when they had briefly slept in the same barracks, and he admired and envied Rudolf's courage, which seemed indomitable.

Brasse, too, could have made more use of his position, now that he had made himself a friend of the SS, but he preferred to play it safe, there in Block 26, not letting his gaze stray outside. He never denied anyone a favor and always shared the goods that came his way, thanks to his photography work—especially the food. He never went further than that, though. He could have been more active in trading, bargaining, and exchanging favors with those above and beneath him, but he never did.

On that evening, he looked at Rudolf and imagined being more like him, but then he shook himself, laughing at his own daydreams. He got to his feet and went over to where the newly-weds were seated, putting his hands on their shoulders.

"It's time for the official photograph, don't you think?"

Friemel and Margarita got up and, making their excuses to their guests, took Edi by the hand and left the table that had been set up in the corridor where newly arrived prisoners usually stood in line, waiting to be registered.

Brasse ushered them into the studio and closed the door behind them.

He felt happy again. Here, he was in charge.

"Now, do just as I ask, and it'll only take a minute."

He had already thought about how to resolve the main difficulty of photographing three people at once instead of the usual single portrait. It was going to be tricky with a fixed photography desk. He took Edi in his arms and sat him in the revolving chair. Then he placed Rudolf on the boy's left and Margarita on the right. He asked the oberkapo to smile at the camera and Margarita to look at her son. The two allowed themselves to be guided by him, but the most well behaved of all was the little boy, who—not at all intimidated—hardly took his eyes off the Zeiss for a second and didn't wriggle or fidget. Just once, he looked away, but he still didn't spoil the composition.

"Are you ready?"

"Ready!"

Brasse took the picture.

"Done! I'll print it tomorrow."

Not long afterward, when the celebrations were over, the bride and groom said good night to their guests, and the nuptial banquet came to an end. The SS had allowed Margarita and Rudolf to spend the first night of their married life in Block 24, the camp brothel, having moved the women who usually lived there elsewhere.

The next morning, in the light of a cold, bright day, Friemel's parents, Margarita, and Edi left the camp and headed straight back to Vienna. Rudolf said goodbye without shedding a single tear, passing his courage on to them, but Brasse, who was with him, knew how much pain he held in his heart.

"What next?" Friemel asked Brasse with a lost look as soon as his family had gone through the camp gate. The photographer shook his head, powerless, and also moved almost to tears. He wasn't at all sure that his friend would ever see his wife and son again.

That afternoon, Brasse set to work printing the wedding portrait. He already knew that the lighting hadn't been perfect. Rudolf's face had been partially in shadow, but he'd done the best he could with the limited number of lamps he had at his disposal. It was still a beautiful photograph, and much more important than that, it was Rudolf and Margarita's wedding album. An Auschwitz wedding. No technical imperfections could diminish that value. It would be a precious testimony, and one day, when he grew up, Edi would scrutinize the picture, searching for traces of an extraordinary story: the story of his parents.

1 6

HE DIDN'T GIVE HIS NAME, AND HE WAS THE ONLY SS
man ever to have come to be photographed not wearing his
uniform. He had arrived wearing a sports jacket with a white shirt
and a tie. His youthful features, ready smile, and shock of unruly
black hair gave him the look of a student. He couldn't be older
than thirty.

Looking at him through the viewfinder, Brasse thought he
must be a lucky man—there was a large gap between his two front
teeth, and Brasse's grandparents had always told him that this was
a sign of good fortune. The man had thanked him politely for the
photograph and disappeared, still smiling.

Now Brasse found himself face-to-face with this individual
again, this time in the Political Department. He'd been summoned

there a few minutes earlier, without warning. Feeling anxious, Brasse had stopped what he was doing immediately and hurried to see Walter. On his arrival, his fears had dissipated just as quickly as they had materialized: there was no danger, and Walter simply wanted to introduce him to somebody—the German who looked like a student, who was now wearing the uniform of an SS Hauptsturmführer.

"Brasse, this is Hauptsturmführer Mengele. You've already met, if I'm not mistaken."

"Yes, sir. I had the pleasure of taking the captain's photograph a few days ago."

Mengele, who had been sitting in an armchair next to Walter's desk, got to his feet and came to greet Brasse. The photographer overcame his hesitation and held out his hand. Mengele shook it firmly, only letting go after a few seconds had passed.

"Herr Brasse, I respect those who work and especially those who work with artistry and precision. I am very pleased with your portrait. You have nothing to learn from your counterparts in Berlin, I assure you. Now, please sit down."

"Thank you, sir."

The photographer took a seat, feeling uneasy, while Walter explained what was going to be required of him.

"Hauptsturmführer Mengele is one of the best doctors in the camp. In fact, he's one of the most promising scientists in the whole of the Reich, and we are honored to have him working here at Auschwitz. He asked for you, Brasse, because he needs your help. And now the doctor himself can explain further."

Brasse turned to Mengele, who spoke in a businesslike manner.

"It's very simple. I want to document my work with complete precision, but I'm no photographer. That's why I intend to send some of my subjects to you to be photographed. I need pictures of a special nature. Do you think that is possible?"

Brasse swallowed. He didn't know what Mengele did and had no idea what he meant by "subjects" or a "special nature," but he couldn't argue with the SS.

He nodded. "I will do everything I can."

The captain smiled and got up to shake Brasse's hand again. "I knew I could count on you. You'll hear more from me soon."

Walter beamed and clapped his hands. "Herr Hauptsturmführer, I'm always pleased when we SS can give one another a hand. The Identification Service now helps out all our comrades in Auschwitz, and this meeting is yet more proof of its usefulness. As for you, Brasse, remember what I said to you: I have great plans for your studio. Thanks to Dr. Mengele, you'll soon understand what I mean. Now go, and leave us alone."

Holding his cap in his hands, the photographer gave a slight bow and retreated to the door. Once outside, he took a deep breath of crisp air before making his way back to Block 26. En route, he came across the penal company. The men, carrying their hoes on their shoulders, were returning from a day spent digging a canal and were exhausted. The sight of them was enough to lighten Brasse's heart, though. Whatever surprise Mengele had in store for him, however vile it might be, it was nothing in comparison to the torment these prisoners were suffering.

As for Walter's grand plans, which always sounded so menacing, Brasse set his jaw: he had survived in Auschwitz for years now, and he wasn't about to give up any time soon. He was willing to play his part in whatever Walter's plans were if it would help him survive. But he didn't want to think about that too much. When he got back to the Identification Service, he plunged himself into his work and quickly forgot about the two SS men.

One evening a few days later, as he was bending over the enlarger, printing photographs of the survivors of the latest convoy of Romani, Brasse heard a knock at the door. He knew that nobody would disturb him without a reason, so he called them in. It was Trałka, deathly pale even in the faint red light of the darkroom.

The young man cleared his throat.

"There's a kapo here," he began. "A woman, with some girls…"

Brasse waited for the end of the sentence, but it didn't come. "Well?"

Trałka was clearly disturbed, and he gestured toward the studio. "They say a certain Dr. Mengele sent them. And they want you."

The photographer stood up from the enlarger and wiped his suddenly sweaty hands on the trousers of his uniform.

"All right. You carry on here."

Brasse walked into the studio calmly, determined not to

betray any emotion despite whatever sight might greet him. He found himself in front of a corpulent German kapo—a woman with blond hair and the black triangle signifying "asocial" sewn onto her chest. A young Polish woman stood next to her, a political prisoner acting as her assistant. Despite her tired and haunted eyes, the young prisoner possessed a quiet beauty that drew Brasse's attention. Near to the two women stood four Jewish girls, all shaking and unsteady on their legs. The oldest must have been fifteen, the youngest no more than twelve. They were so thin that their uniforms hung off their bodies. They gazed around like baby sparrows begging for compassion. Brasse looked from them to their guardians and back again. He didn't know what to say or do.

"Are you the photographer?" the kapo asked.

"Yes."

She pointed at the girls. "Dr. Mengele wants you to take their pictures."

Brasse took a deep breath, trying to control his anguish. "Did he give any specific instructions?"

The woman nodded. "He wants three full-length shots. He used those exact words: 'full-length.' He wants them from the front, from behind, and in profile. And they must be naked. Is that clear?"

"Naked? Why?"

The woman gave a coarse laugh. "I'm not the doctor. You do as you're told and don't ask questions."

The photographer looked at the girls, embarrassed. They

huddled together under his gaze like a brood of chicks wanting their mother. He opened his mouth to reassure them but couldn't say a word.

So he turned to the political prisoner and spoke to her in Polish. "Help them undress."

The girls understood his words—they, too, were Polish. They began to tremble and cry, slowly, silently, as if they only had a few tears to shed.

"What's the matter?" he asked the woman.

"They're ashamed of undressing in front of a man."

Brasse thought for a moment. "Wait. I've got an idea."

He went over to a large screen that Walter had procured for him from Warsaw, which was used for portraits of the SS. He pushed it over to the girls.

"Undress behind there. No one will watch."

He thought quickly. How to go about this? He cursed Walter under his breath. The studio was equipped for taking portraits, not group photographs. Now Mengele was exploiting Walter's naivete and sending him people for full-length photographs. There was only one thing he could do.

"Tadek!" he called out.

Brodka, who'd been busying himself with the boxes for the negatives, came over.

"Get me the portable camera. We'll use that. We'll do without the Zeiss for once."

Then, taking the little Contax usually used for outdoor shots,

Brasse prepared to photograph Mengele's "subjects." His consternation increased as he waited for the girls to appear. He could hear their high, twittering voices as they undressed with the help of the Polish guard, who spoke to them in a motherly tone.

He didn't want to see them. They had broken his heart even with their uniforms on. He didn't want to see them naked. He was tempted to pass the task over to Brodka or Trałka, but he couldn't. It wasn't that he was afraid that he would be found out—nobody, not even Walter, would ever know if he delegated this job—rather that he couldn't make his team do such a terrible thing. He was the chief photographer, and it was up to him to handle it. He gripped the camera tightly and stayed where he was.

Finally, the girls came out into the open, taking small steps and holding hands. They lined up in front of the backdrop. Their eyes expressed their infinite shame, but they didn't make the slightest move to cover their private parts. They clearly knew what was expected of them. The Polish woman saw that the kapo had disappeared somewhere, probably to smoke a cigarette, and she turned calmly to the girls.

"Now, do as Herr Brasse tells you. Don't worry. It'll be fine."

The photographer bent down to peer through the viewfinder and looked at the girls one by one. They were starving. They had been for some time. Their ribs were sticking out, their stomachs and thighs so sunken that he could have encircled them with his hands, and their little legs and knees curved inward. He had to wipe away his tears. They had been shaved all over but roughly, and it looked as though their hair and skin had been ripped off violently.

Then he noticed something else: they were two sets of twins. The first and fourth were taller and darker. The second and third were shorter, with paler skin. He wondered fleetingly what interest Mengele could possibly have in twins but gave up seeking an answer. He didn't want to be the one to adjust their position, as he usually did with his "clients," to pose them correctly. He gave instructions to the Polish prisoner instead, and she was the one who pulled the girls' shoulders upward, lifted their chins, and straightened their arms by their sides. When they were ready, he took the photographs.

Three of them.

One from the front, one behind, and one in profile.

"That's it," he said. "You can get dressed now."

He could see that they were pleased to have followed his orders without making any mistakes. As they went back behind the screen, he turned to the Polish woman.

"What does he do with them?" he asked.

The woman didn't reply, pretending not to have heard, but Brasse caught her by the arm.

"What's your name?" he pressed.

She pulled away violently. "Let me go. Stefańska, but everyone calls me Baśka."

"Where are you from?"

"Kraków."

"I'm from Żywiec—not far from there."

The woman looked at him hesitantly, and he felt a surge of anger. He took her arm again and shook her.

"Look, I'm a prisoner just like you. Why are you afraid? Tell me what he does to those girls!"

The woman looked down, and when she raised her eyes again, her hesitation had given way to the same distress that Brasse had seen in the eyes of the girls.

She shrugged. "I don't know."

"I don't believe you. Is it a secret?"

"It's a secret. But I really don't know anything."

"You haven't seen anything?"

"I've seen him measuring them and weighing them, and he records every detail about their health. I haven't seen or heard anything else. The kapo knows more…"

But Brasse had no intention of talking to the German "asocial."

He sat down, worn out.

A thought occurred to him, and he jumped to his feet and went into the darkroom to get some bread. He brought it into the studio and passed it to the Polish woman.

"Hide it. And give it to them. Understood?"

She nodded silently and concealed the bread in her jacket.

The girls reappeared, as shaky as they had been when they arrived, still holding hands, their uniforms hanging off them. Baśka stroked their hair and ordered them to follow her. They left the studio without looking back, without even glancing at Brasse. *They were like lifeless dolls*, he thought. Like the mechanical toys he used to see in the shops of Żywiec when he was little. Those dolls were destined to be pampered by rich children who would play with them until their mechanisms broke, and then they'd end up tossed into a trunk in the attic. You can do anything to dolls. Nobody complains.

Brasse wiped his hands on his trousers again. They were still sweating.

He was filled with anguish and felt dirty.

The little Jewish girls had put him in contact with Mengele. He hadn't touched them, but something of the doctor had passed through them and seized him by the throat.

He decided not to print the photographs himself. He would leave the job to Wawrzyniak and wouldn't check the results. He was sure that the Hauptsturmführer would still be pleased with their work.

17

KEEP ON FORGETTING. NEVER STOP FORGETTING. Every day, delete what you saw the day before. Leave every hour behind you, bury it in darkness. That was the rule for survival. Brasse also forced himself to close his eyes to the future: no dreams, no illusions. He must live in the moment and survive like that.

Over the next few days, he strove to forget, as he always did. The photographs of the four little Jewish girls were delivered to Mengele, who didn't fail to pass on his compliments for the excellent work. Walter was delighted, and everyone in Block 26 saw that for some reason, the collaboration between the Erkennungsdienst and Dr. Mengele was considered by their superiors to be of great strategic importance.

They talked about it one morning, as fellow prisoners and as colleagues.

"It's better for us if there's more work to do," Wawrzyniak said. "Sooner or later, the work doing portraits, copies, and enlargements for the SS will dry up."

There was a pause in the discussion. There was no need to elaborate. They all knew full well that if there was less work, their number would be reduced immediately.

Brasse looked at his assistant. He was right, of course, but still Brasse couldn't help thinking how it was Wawrzyniak who had printed the photo of the Jewish twins. He had seen their terrified gaze, with its mixture of fear and hope that someone would help them, that a merciful hand would cover them, and he had fixed it onto the photographic paper. And yet here he was, saying quite naturally that this work was good news, seemingly with no sense of guilt.

Brasse tried to chase away these thoughts. He glanced around. Brodka was looking down and nodding at Wawrzyniak's wise words, but perhaps he, too, was remembering the moment when he had been so horrified by the sight of the girls.

"Well, let's get back to work!"

Brasse never needed to chivvy his colleagues along, but he did it instinctively, to stop himself from lingering over these painful thoughts.

The kommando went back to their various tasks.

Brasse had been in the middle of retouching a photograph

of a German soldier in civilian clothes with his fiancée, a smiling blond in traditional Bavarian costume. He focused on the image and began to improve the definition of the oval outline of her face with tiny, delicate strokes.

All of a sudden, the image of Baśka, the young political prisoner who had helped him comfort the four young girls, came into his mind. It was like a flash of light from a hidden part of his heart. He wished she were there so he could talk to her about what had happened. She had seemed so human. Her prisoner's defenses had held up only for a short time against his insistence when he had wanted to know what Mengele did with the girls. Then she had stroked their hair.

He closed his eyes and tried to conjure up her voice saying his name: "Wilhelm..."

He imagined her smiling at him, looking lovingly at him, touching him. He remembered that she was beautiful and realized that even in those highly charged moments when he had looked at her, he had discovered her in the way a man discovers a woman. He hadn't been able to acknowledge this emotion at the time. He thought about it now, though—again and again. Perhaps to help him forget the painful memory of the four twittering girls.

His hand began to tremble. He swore. He'd made a mistake. The German fiancée, radiant in the sun, was now marked by his distraction. He'd be in trouble if the soldier saw the damage. He tried to gather the self-possession needed to repair his error, but it wasn't easy. The juxtaposition of Baśka's beauty and humanity, the little girls with their desperate need for love, and his own longing for peace destabilized him. These were thoughts and feelings he was no longer used to having, dangerous ideas that must be pushed away.

Freedom from his torment came in the form of Myszkowski, who had come back from a job he'd been asked to do in Block 20.

"There's trouble on the way," his colleague announced.

They all looked at him worriedly.

"An epidemic's broken out. Another one."

Myszkowski put the Contax down on the table, sat in his chair, and rubbed his face with his hand. He wore the tired look that came over him whenever he came back with horrifying images to develop and print.

"I've been taking photographs of ill people for the doctors."

Brasse picked up the camera and weighed it in his hand.

"What sort of epidemic?"

"Typhus is what they're saying. The ones who've caught it have a fever and spots on their skin. You can see them in the photos."

Wawrzyniak said what they were all thinking. "Is it serious? Is it contagious?"

"If you're already weak, it's fatal. And yes, I asked whether it's infectious. The doctors say it's passed on by lice."

This encouraging information was met with a sigh of relief: they all had enough to eat, and the places they ate and slept were fairly clean and well aerated.

Brasse thought to himself that since they'd almost stopped

Wilhelm Brasse as a young man.

Brasse in 1938, before his
imprisonment at Auschwitz.

Brasse in 2009 at home in Żywiec, Poland, with some of the many thousands
of photographs he risked his life to save before Auschwitz was liberated.

Josef Mengele (1911–79), the SS doctor at Auschwitz-Birkenau who led the Nazis' pseudomedical research projects. He wanted all his experiments to be documented meticulously and requested that Brasse photograph some of his subjects.

Carl Clauberg (1898–1957), SS member and doctor at Auschwitz. Gynecological experiments led by Clauberg at the concentration camp were supposedly aimed at developing new methods of sterilization. Like Mengele, he used Brasse to document his tortures.

Brasse's portrait of Untersturmführer Maximilian Grabner (1905–47). Grabner was head of the Political Department at Auschwitz and the direct superior of Bernhard Walter, chief of the Identification Service.

Rudolf Friemel (1907–44), Austrian communist and Auschwitz political prisoner, was the only inmate at the camp permitted to marry during their detention. Brasse captured this wedding portrait of Friemel with his new wife, Margarita Ferrer, and their son, Edi.

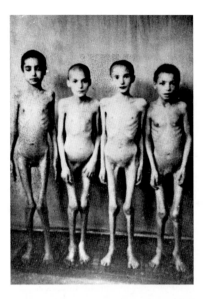

Four Jewish girls, photographed by Brasse under Mengele's orders. The occasion marked the beginning of Mengele's exploitation of Brasse's photography skills.

Jewish prisoners after alighting from a train arriving in Auschwitz, May 1944. One of many outdoor shots the SS ordered the Identification Service to take, which helped document the extermination camp's "efficiency."

Prisoner selection (*above*) and the sorting of personal belongings taken from newly arrived prisoners (*below*), May 1944.

Between 1940 and 1945, Brasse photographed 40,000–50,000 prisoners during the registration process. Three images were taken on each occasion: a profile shot, a full-on portrait without the prisoner wearing headgear, and a three-quarter view in which they wore their cap or headscarf.

Czesława Kwoka (1928–43) was assaulted by Kapo Wacek Ruski just before Brasse took her portrait. Imprisoned in 1942 and registered under the number 26947, Czesława was a Polish political prisoner (PPole).

Krystyna Trzesniewska (1929–43). Another Polish political prisoner photographed by Brasse, Krystyna was taken to Auschwitz in 1942 with her father and was registered under the number 27129.

Written signs in Brasse's portraits detailed where each individual came from, their identity number, and why they were in Auschwitz.

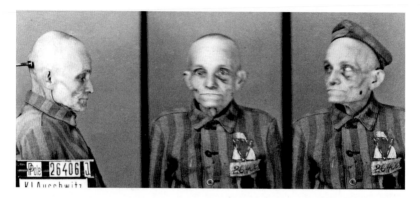

Imprisoned in March 1942, Aron Loewi (1879–1942) was registered under the number 26406 as a PPole (Polish political prisoner), with the addition of the letter J to signal his Jewish identity.

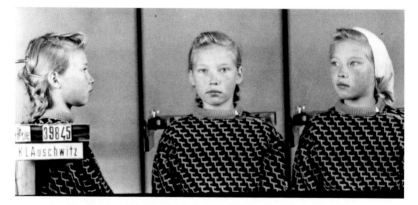

Young Polish political prisoner Rozalia Kowalczyk, registered under the number 39845.

Birkenau, Poland, May 1944. Women and children on their way to gas chamber number 4.

Birkenau, Poland, May 1944. Jewish prisoners wait near gas chamber number 4 before being sent to their deaths.

Jozef Pysz, imprisoned in July 1940. Number 1420 PPole.
He was one of the earliest prisoners in the camp.

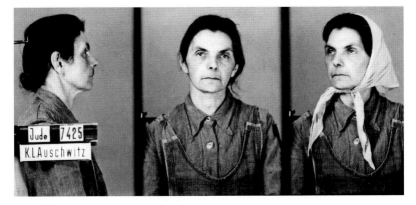

Unknown prisoner, imprisoned in May 1942. Number 7425 Jude
(Jewish). Women had begun to arrive in the camp in March 1942.

Stefania Stiebler. Imprisoned in June 1942, Stiebler was a Yugoslavian political prisoner and Jew—7602 Pol:J—who worked in the camp offices and played an active role in the resistance movement.

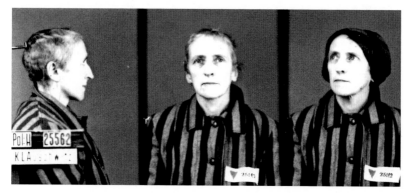

Unknown Dutch political prisoner 25562, imprisoned in 1942.

Men in camp uniform pronounced fit for labor, May 1944.

Jewish women marching to their barracks in Birkenau, May 1944.

Jewish women wearing camp uniform, May 1944.

Gottlieb Wagner, prisoner number 17850, categorized as Aso
(or "asocial," as the Nazis termed those imprisoned for not fitting
their narrow definition of socially acceptable behavior).

Stanisław Watycha (1906–41). Imprisoned in August 1941, number 20107 PPole. Watycha, a teacher, was shot November 11, 1941—Polish Independence Day—along with a further 150 prisoners in one of the first executions involving Block 11's infamous "Death Wall."

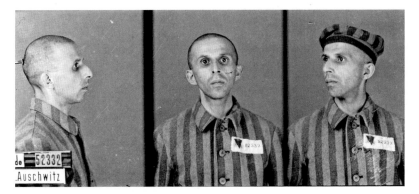

Leo Israel Vogelbaum (1904–42). Imprisoned in July 1942, number 52332 Jude (Jewish).

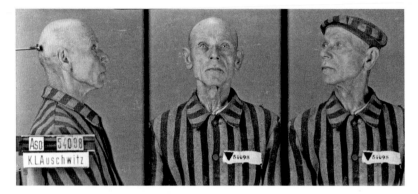

August Wittek (1874–1942). Imprisoned in July
1942, number 54098 Aso ("asocial").

Franz Slokau. Imprisoned in August 1942, number
57860 Pol:S (Slovenian political prisoner).

It is not possible to know exactly which prisoner registration photographs
were taken by Brasse himself and which were taken by other members of
the *Erkennungsdienst*, though many credited to Brasse can be found in the
Auschwitz-Birkenau State Museum's permanent exhibit in Block 6.

photographing dozens and dozens of prisoners each day, the risk of catching lice from one of them had dropped significantly. He didn't say anything, though. The others were already feeling reassured.

"Do they want these photographs straightaway?"

He already knew the answer: the doctors in Block 20 had received the order to document this emergency swiftly. A report for the authorities needed to be ready by that evening, to be sent off to Berlin. Hearing Myszkowski talk about the doctors who had given him the instruction, Brasse could barely resist asking him if Mengele had been among them. He wanted to forget about the man, but he also carried the hope that this health crisis would force the doctor to neglect his research.

"Right," he said, immediately practical. "Tadek, stop what you're doing and develop them straightaway."

Walter came over in the afternoon. He was tense and wanted information about the photographs.

"They'll all be ready by five o'clock," Brasse assured him.

At that moment, the pictures were hanging up to dry. Naked bodies, shivering, exposed to the cold, emaciated, made still more defenseless by illness. And covered in spots. Some of the sores had been photographed close up, and they were oozing pus.

"Sickening!" Walter spat. He was disgusted and angry. And clearly afraid.

Brasse made no comment, but Walter didn't hold back. "We won't be able to treat many of them, but that's not the point. This is an illness you can catch just by standing near the prisoners. My colleagues are keeping their distance, but being careful isn't enough."

Brasse didn't allow any emotion to show on his face, but he reflected on how strange it was that the prisoners had suddenly—without meaning to and without lifting a finger—become a mortal danger to their jailers.

Then he thought of Baśka. He saw her taking care of the emaciated girls and remembered her eyes, full of despair. He realized that she was in danger.

"What's wrong with you?" Walter was staring at him, annoyed because Brasse wasn't listening to him.

Brasse stiffened. "Nothing, Herr Hauptscharführer."

"Are you feeling sympathy for those people, or are you worried about what might happen to our collaborators?"

Brasse could lie, but Walter would realize. He was just there, an inch away, gazing at him with impatience and hatred.

"I'm afraid for myself, as we all are," he replied, looking down as though confessing to a crime.

The German was satisfied with this.

"Quite. For the prisoners, death is a liberation. But as for us, dear Brasse, as for *us*," he said with emphasis, forcing Brasse to meet his eye, "we must not die like them. We are intended for a different destiny, and you believe that too. So we will limit, as far as we can, any visits to prisoners living in poor sanitary conditions."

Brasse thought immediately of the women in Birkenau who weren't allowed to wash. Of all the women.

"In the meantime, let's have confidence in our excellent doctors. Go on with your work, Herr Brasse, and don't be afraid. If you do fall ill, you will receive the best of care."

As he said this, he placed a friendly hand on Brasse's shoulder. Brasse didn't pull away but simply lowered his eyes.

At five o'clock, Maltz appeared. He hadn't been seen all day. He took the photographs and tucked them into an envelope labeled with the name of the illness. He made sure to touch them only with the tips of his fingers, as though contagion could be spread through the pictures themselves. Brasse and Myszkowski watched him, respectful and expressionless. He suddenly looked up at them with a nasty, pleased smile.

"Do you want some good news?"

They didn't know what to say, and the kapo made the most of their surprise.

"Guess who's come down with the fever?"

They waited in suspense. They couldn't imagine who the kapo could hate so much that he'd be pleased to see them fall ill.

"But if I tell you, don't celebrate too much as soon as I leave the room. At the moment, the kapos are most at risk, so I want a bit of respect, even from you, you lucky, ungrateful bastards!"

His mood had changed abruptly, and he was now furious. Brasse and Myszkowski remained impassive, but they feared the consequences of these mood swings.

"Well, one of the ones who's got it worst is Ruski. That devil's in Block 20, covered in sores. That's what you get for fucking the Jews!"

And he laughed—a horrible laugh, and an envious one.

There had long been rumors that Ruski, the brutal killer and kapo of the penal colony, raped women and girls he happened to come across, taking them down to the bunker of Block 11. Myszkowski managed a smile to humor Maltz. It even had a touch of complicity with the kapo's resentment of Ruski's freedom to indulge his desires.

Brasse didn't smile. He was thinking of the Jewish girls. He was thinking of Baśka.

"What?" Maltz barked. "Are you sorry for that devil?"

The kapo was eyeing him with hatred and suspicion. Brasse could read his thoughts: what if, when he recovered, Ruski got to know that Maltz had rejoiced in the news of his illness?

"So, Brasse. You wouldn't want him dead, our dear Ruski? Go on, say it. You have my permission."

A long, tense silence followed. A calculation of the possible consequences of each answer. And then the inevitable truth.

"Yes. I'd like him dead. But they'll look after him well, and people recover from this illness if they're not already too weak. And Ruski is one of the strongest in here."

Maltz's eyes narrowed. He was considering something very carefully. Then, without warning, he began to smile again.

"We'll see," he concluded serenely. And he left without another word.

Over the next few days, life in the camp proceeded at a slower pace. The roll calls still took place and work units passed by with bowed heads, but people spoke even less than they usually did and kept as far away from one another as possible. The kapos bellowed as usual, but when they hit prisoners with their sticks, they drew back immediately, leaving their victims bent double on the ground, winded, or kneeling with their head in their hands, their final strength spent sobbing.

The state of emergency lasted only a few days, then the epidemic stopped spreading so quickly, and word went around that the doctors in Block 20 had been very well organized: those prisoners too weak to recover had been killed immediately without even being sent to the hospital, and those the doctors wanted to save had been well looked after.

During this time, the prisoners in Block 26 often saw the wretched men of the penal company passing by, but Ruski was never with them.

Then, one morning, Maltz brought them the news, as triumphant as if he'd had a promotion.

"Gone!" he announced. "I knew that Polish shit had trodden on someone's toes."

And it was true: among the victims of the fever was Wacek Ruski, the murderer, the man Brasse had implored to have mercy on his friends from Żywiec and not kill them too horribly.

"They let him die," Maltz said. "You should have seen him lying there, a complete wreck, on a sodden straw mattress. He could hardly breathe. And the best part is that he must have realized that they'd decided to abandon him. He kept gazing around in desperation, hoping that someone would come and look after him. He thought he was all-powerful, and nobody lifted a finger to help him!"

Brasse received this news without any particular emotion. The death of one of the worst killers in the camp didn't improve their situation and only offered brief and bitter consolation to the wretches in Block 11. The Nazis certainly wouldn't replace Ruski with a kind, gentle kapo.

Perhaps Maltz hoped to be appointed to that position, but he wasn't. He stopped celebrating quickly and vented his anger by kicking Brodka in a quiet moment.

18

"What's she doing?"

Stanisław Trałka had looked up from his work and glanced out of the window.

"Who?" asked Brasse absentmindedly.

"That woman. I've seen her before but I can't remember when. She's standing there looking at our block... Now she's going."

The photographer made his way to the window and saw a female prisoner walk quickly away from the block and join a group of about a dozen very young, thin girls several feet from the studio. For some reason, she had gone on ahead by herself. A shout from the kapo had brought her back, and she was receiving a telling-off in silence. She had broken the rule of the group by going ahead alone and stopping to look at the studio windows.

It was Baśka.

Where are you running to? Brasse wondered. *What did you hope to see?*

The girls were joined by two other prisoners—twins—who were holding hands. They all began to walk toward Block 26.

"It's the next group of girls to photograph for Mengele," Brasse announced to the others.

Immediately, two members of the kommando moved the backdrop into place so that the girls could undress behind it. When Mengele had sent word to Brasse that new subjects were about to arrive, Brasse had feared that he would once again find himself faced with these little innocents, but he had also hoped to see Baśka again.

The girls entered the studio and stood in a line. This time, everyone knew what to do: in Auschwitz, everything quickly became a procedure to be followed. As the girls—all sets of twins again—were positioned correctly, Baśka kept her eyes lowered, but several times, Brasse had the feeling she was watching him. Or was that just a hope?

He tried to think of a way to speak to her without arousing the suspicion of the kapo, who remained in the room and was keeping a watchful eye on them all.

When the photographs had been taken, however, Baśka surprised him by addressing him openly.

"Herr Brasse, Dr. Mengele ordered me to tell you that he will be sending more subjects tomorrow. More twins. And…"

She hesitated briefly. He looked at her in silence, with the respect required of a prisoner who had received instructions from an SS official. But he looked straight into her eyes. Baśka sensed that he was making the most of this brief exchange to memorize her features.

"Then other kinds of prisoners will come," she continued. "Still from Birkenau. To be photographed naked, full length, and in three positions. Like today."

"We are at Dr. Mengele's service," Brasse said, trying to smile and insert a little irony into his tone.

Baśka responded with a brief smile.

When the girls had all left, Brodka replied to Brasse's silent question. "She speaks very good German and works as Mengele's secretary."

Brasse didn't ask his colleague who he was talking about. There was no point disguising his interest.

"She's…beautiful," Brodka said.

Brasse shrugged and went back to work.

Two days later, Mengele sent them a new kind of prisoner to photograph. Under the curious gazes of the whole team, ten people with dwarfism lined up in the corridor—some male and some female. Even Brasse was surprised to see them. They were different from dwarfs he'd seen before: Mengele had chosen only those who had torsos of ordinary size and short legs and arms.

Nobody said anything.

Brasse photographed them all, one by one, after waiting for them to undress behind the backdrop screen. They carried themselves with dignity despite having some difficulty with their movements. Brasse took great care with their portraits, as though they were esteemed guests.

Two sisters and a brother were among the group, and Mengele's instructions were to photograph them together so the similarity between them could be seen.

The kapo was outside with the others, and encouraged by the kindness of Brasse and his team, the three siblings relaxed enough to smile and talk a little. The man accepted a cigarette.

"We're Jewish, from Budapest," he said. "They arrested us, and we've been kept together. We only hope it lasts."

"Did you used to live together?"

"We lived and worked together, and before the war, we were doing all right. She plays the violin, she plays the guitar," he said, pointing to his sisters, "and I sing. We earned enough to live on by playing in cabarets. People would see us coming onto the stage and laugh and make the same old jokes about dwarfs. We silenced them with our music. They never loved us or respected us, but nobody ever dreamed it would go from teasing us to putting us in a camp. The Nazis haven't got a sense of humor, though, you know…"

"Be quiet!"

One of the sisters was afraid that the walls might have ears.

The brother finished his cigarette.

"Take some more," Brasse said, offering the packet.

"Thank you, you're very kind. The doctor is kind too. He just wants to study us. He weighs us, measures us, asks us questions about our childhood, our parents... Perhaps the Germans are afraid we're contagious. It's the only explanation. But I don't get it. They're the masters of the world—what have they got to fear from us?"

Their conversation was interrupted by the kapo calling them back.

One of the sisters stood to attention instinctively. Her brother looked at her with sad irony.

"It's no use showing how obedient you are. There's no hope for us."

He said it calmly, with dignity. Then he inhaled the smoke of his cigarette deep into his lungs. Brasse found himself thinking that he really did look like a condemned man having his final smoke and felt an overwhelming despair.

"Goodbye," said the youngest sister as she left.

That evening, looking at his portrait of the trio, Brasse tried to imagine them playing and singing. He thought of them in a smoke-filled club, in a semidarkness that relaxed people's eyes and allowed them to unwind and let go without fear of being recognized. He saw the audience laughing, reassured by the differences between themselves and the three unfortunates on the stage as they walked forward awkwardly to make a clumsy bow to the darkness before them.

Before the war, he'd been to a few such cabarets, but he'd

never seen dwarfs performing. He wondered whether he, too, would have laughed and nudged the person next to him. Now he wouldn't dream of it.

The siren for roll call sounded. Brasse left Block 26 and fell in line like an obedient prisoner. The air was freezing; it was sure to be a pitiless winter. The weakest prisoners, rigid with cold, were already shifting their feet in their worn-out shoes, trying to warm them up. *None of these poor souls who are feeling the cold already, so soon, will live to see spring*, thought Brasse. And he realized how knowledgeable he had become, how even the slightest details of the prisoners' behavior told him something about them. He had become an expert in predicting their destiny.

He replied when his name was called, waited for the order to disperse, then turned and headed back to Block 26 to finish his work.

"Wilhelm!"

Brodka grasped his arm and led him to one side. He looked alarmed, his eyes signaling an urgent problem.

"What's going on?"

"You see that prisoner there?" his friend replied, pointing at a young man who was standing hesitantly, watching them, while the prisoners filed back to their barracks.

Brasse nodded.

"It's a friend of mine from Lwów. He's just arrived, and his father's got a photography studio. Can we try to get him to join our group?"

The photographer looked at the young man, who was

watching them, full of hope. He tried to think, but Brodka had already worked it all out.

"You could tell Walter that we've got lots of retouching to do. He's a young photographer, but he's very good at that kind of work."

They looked each other in the eye, acknowledging in silence the unspoken question. Why would such a young photographer be an expert in retouching?

"All right," Brasse said. "I'll talk to Walter tomorrow."

The following day, two SS men who had obtained permission from their superiors to go to the Identification Service to have their portraits taken had to wait, incredulous, while Brasse finished taking photographs of another group of dwarfs. When the dwarfs had gone, filing past the two SS men with their heads down and holding their breath, the two officers insisted that the chair be cleaned carefully before they sat on it.

The photographer treated them with deference, still considering how to tackle the conversation with Walter.

As though Brasse had called him, Walter entered the studio at that moment and replied pleasantly to the greetings of his subordinates. He stayed to watch how things were going, then saluted and made to leave.

"Herr Hauptscharführer?"

"Yes?"

There was a slight note of impatience in the officer's voice, but Brasse didn't give up.

"I have a request to make regarding the operation of the studio."

Walter glanced quickly at the two SS men, not wanting to appear too accommodating in front of them.

"Is it urgent?"

"Yes. I wouldn't dare to inconvenience you otherwise."

The two Germans, having finished, saluted and left.

"What is it?"

"Herr Walter, as you know, our workload is increasing—especially the number of portraits that officers and soldiers ask us to retouch."

"So?"

Walter was on his guard, his good humor having vanished entirely.

"I've heard that a prisoner has just arrived at the camp—a Polish man…" Here, Brasse paused ever so slightly, as if to emphasize that they were talking about a "mere" Pole. "His father has a photography studio in Lwów, and he has learned several techniques, especially retouching. He would be useful to us, if you would give your permission."

For a long time, Walter looked at Brasse, who held his gaze.

"News travels fast, I see. I myself hadn't heard anything about this new arrival. What's your candidate's name?"

"Edward Josefsberg."

"Will you answer for him?"

"I'll answer for him. We can take him on for a trial period, and I'll assess his abilities. I'll teach him a little, if need be."

The German interrupted with a gesture of annoyance.

"Very well, very well, Herr Brasse. I will have faith in you. And I also understand your haste. For all we know, your colleague may already be on a list of people to be eliminated. Bring him to me as soon as you can. Introduce him to me, and if all goes well, we will add him to the team."

"Thank you, Herr Walter. With your permission, I'll have him come here this afternoon."

As soon as Walter had left the room, Brodka hurried to call his friend. Half an hour later, the young man arrived.

"Everyone calls me Edek," he said.

"Edek's fine by us," said Brasse, shaking his hand. The young man was standing stiffly, almost to attention. Brodka must have exaggerated the extent to which his salvation depended on Brasse.

"Do you really know how to do high-quality retouching?"

"Yes…" Josefsberg glanced at Brodka, who smiled encouragingly.

"All right," Brasse said curtly. "You'll learn, with a bit of patience."

An hour later, Walter arrived and scrutinized the newcomer warily.

"You're a mess."

Josefsberg's uniform was indeed a sorry sight, ragged and stained.

"And you stink. How long has it been since you had a wash?"

"Well, I… We…"

"You haven't got lice, have you?"

Embarrassment threatened to overwhelm the young man. He could see the German was afraid because of the recent epidemic.

"I...don't think so."

"Brasse, get this boy a new uniform, and take him to have a shower straightaway."

A member of the kommando ran off to get the items of clothing as quickly as possible. Josefsberg waited patiently, wandering around the studio and observing the others at work. When the clothes arrived, he and Brasse walked around Block 26 to the showers at the back. Brasse held the new uniform, and Josefsberg followed him trustingly. The sun was shining, barely producing any warmth, but a pleasant sight nonetheless. Brasse felt good in his role as a protector.

"Get undressed."

Josefsberg didn't hesitate and was soon standing naked in front of Brasse. And in that moment, his savior's world collapsed around him.

"My God, Edek! You're circumcised!"

Josefsberg blushed. "Wilhelm..."

"Are you Jewish? Do they know? Come on. Tell me!"

"No! I'm not Jewish. It was an operation for a tight foreskin, not a circumcision!"

Brasse looked again at Josefsberg's penis. Walter hated Jews: if he even so much as suspected that Brasse had duped him, that he'd lied to him to save a Jew...

"You must believe me, please!"

The photographer opened the door to the shower block and looked outside. There was no one around. He bowed his head, thought quickly, and closed the door again.

"Listen. I don't have to believe anything at all. You're circumcised, and that's that. That's enough for them to have us executed before you can blather out your story about tight foreskins. So listen to me: every time we come here to shower, make sure you hide behind us. Nobody must see your penis. Do you understand?"

"Yes."

"We'd all be doomed."

"Yes, yes."

The boy was trembling now, with fear and cold.

"Have a shower and get dressed straightaway."

Brasse waited outside while Josefsberg did as he was told. A group of SS passed by, and he saluted respectfully, but it seemed to him that one of them was looking at him curiously, as though he were beginning to feel suspicious. No, he must have been imagining it. As far as that soldier was concerned, Brasse was transparent, a nothing.

The sky was blue and clear, barely darkened by the first shadow of evening, as limpid as the truth. As the soldiers walked away, Brasse imagined himself shouting, "Hey! I've got a Jew here! But I'll pretend he's Polish like me, and I'll trick you all!"

Absurd thoughts, and dangerous ones. He must stay focused, now more than ever. Suddenly, his sense of exaltation had completely disappeared.

Damn it, he thought. *The first prisoner I take a risk on—who I wanted to save even though it meant having to cover up for his incompetence—is apparently a Jew. An indefensible Jew.*

How long could this last?

19

"Herr Brasse is a true expert. He's taken perfect photographs for my experiments. I couldn't do without him."

Brasse listened to these compliments without batting an eyelid. Walter, on the other hand, looked at him with the satisfaction of a manager receiving praise for his successful team. It was plain to see that Mengele was sincere. Sincere and, as always, kind and attentive.

"I can't take all the credit," Brasse volunteered. "I owe a lot to the efficiency of the whole kommando."

The doctor was clearly impressed by these words.

"You are too humble. Don't underestimate yourself. It seems to me that your colleagues help you with their technical skill, but you are the artist. To have recorded the physical details and even the characters of my subjects so very well, you must have an extraordinary sensitivity."

"It's no surprise that this young man has German blood in his veins. Pure German blood," said Walter, evidently seeking the expert researcher's approval with these words.

Brasse said nothing. He was thinking about the fact that Mengele seemed to wield increasing authority within the camp. Walter's attitude toward him was the clearest indication of this.

"Yes, I can see that," the doctor said. He began to observe Brasse very carefully. He took a step toward him. "These regular, open features, the well-defined chin, the wide forehead, the energetic expression, the clear eyes... Smile, please."

Brasse did as he was told.

"You see these small dimples that form next to his mouth when he smiles?"

Walter nodded, and Mengele pointed to this phenomenon as though he were giving a lecture. He was very serious.

"They are the visible trace of a natural, dynamic predisposition that nothing can repress. This man's whole morphology, his whole body, shows the proportions and vigor of a healthy nature because it is the realization of a positive genetic project."

Taking another step toward Brasse, Mengele began an even closer observation.

"It would be interesting to measure the circumference of the skull and evaluate the bone structure."

"Herr Brasse is Aryan, there's no doubt about it. Your

observations confirm that the efforts I have made for him have not been misplaced, Doctor."

By now, the two men were talking about Brasse as though he weren't there, as though they were calculating the value of an object.

"Efforts?" asked Mengele, surprised. "What sort of efforts?"

"It's clear that he must unite with us and share our mission. Perhaps you can convince him, show him that his destiny is written in his body, in the depths of his eyes. Stop him insisting that he's Polish and bragging about his ties to the Slavic race, which are simply a sentimental attachment to his mother."

"Is that what he says?" Mengele was full of the curiosity of a researcher. He turned to Brasse. "You say you are Polish because of your affection for your mother? Explain."

Brasse was confused. For a moment, he considered saying nothing. They could decide for themselves what the right answer was. They would do whatever they wanted with him, as indeed they already were.

"Well?"

"Herr Mengele, I feel myself to be Polish. I grew up here. So did my father, who, you say, had German blood."

"It isn't a guess, Herr Brasse. It's an objective scientific fact. Learn to take more notice of that than of your emotions!" Mengele's politeness had melted away. Then, just as quickly, it reappeared. "Go on."

Brasse glanced at Walter, but his superior was simply looking at him in silence, impassive.

"I was saying, Herr Mengele, that my father served Poland as though it were his mother country. That's why he fought against the Bolsheviks in 1921."

"But that doesn't mean anything! The circumstances of history may interfere with the development of a genetically predetermined personality, but it is this personality that creates all our destinies. And your father demonstrates it: when he was attacked by the malign power of an inferior race, he acted according to his racial instinct, saying that he was defending his country. Don't you realize that?"

"I don't know…"

"Are you a Communist?"

"No, I'm not a Communist."

"Of course you're not. You can't be a Communist. You are a patriot and a brave man, exactly as your blood dictates."

Mengele was satisfied with his own conclusion.

Walter swelled with pride. "It's as I said. Soon Herr Brasse will admit the obvious. And that's why we allow him to survive."

Mengele agreed. "Good. I intend to study this man further in a future phase of my research. Now I can simply say that his work is useful to us and that he does his work much better than anybody could who was acting through pure obligation."

"Yes, that's true. This is the best confirmation of my expectations."

The two men turned their backs on Brasse, who looked at the floor. He would have liked to sit down, close his eyes, and not feel afraid anymore. But he stayed where he was, standing there like a schoolboy who doesn't know if the teacher and the principal have finished telling him off.

The SS men seemed to be coming to an agreement about something.

"With your permission, Herr Hauptscharführer, I would like to suggest that Herr Brasse can now document real medical experiments and not simply take photographs of the subjects being studied."

"Make whatever arrangements science requires, Herr Hauptsturmführer," Walter told the doctor.

Satisfied with this, Mengele took his cap and made to leave, but first he smiled politely at Brasse.

"Goodbye, Herr Brasse. I would like to thank you once again for your invaluable contribution."

Brasse stood stock-still, waiting.

"Don't let doubts get the better of you," Mengele said. "We are working for the future. Biological determinism is the truth that guides the universe. We will perfect our race and build a humanity free from weakness and illness. Our children will thank us for this and will honor us as gods. Indeed, that is what we are. God doesn't exist, Herr Brasse, if you will excuse my frankness. And do you know why I'm convinced of that? Because I have the proof, each day, that we are the gods. We are the deciders of our own destiny, we are the ones shaping the world, we are the masters of time. Today, we're only powerful; soon, we'll be both powerful and knowledgeable. We're on the brink of great discoveries, you'll see."

Brasse hesitated. He didn't know whether he should say something to show that he agreed or at least show that he had understood.

"Don't rack your brains trying to understand it all now. You'll understand, little by little. And eventually, you'll see it with your own eyes. Because you'll be there, in this new world. Do you understand?"

It was a promise of survival, even though it was expressed as a threat.

Walter nodded. "Yes, Herr Brasse, you will be there. Providing, of course, that we can solve your little problem."

The two men finally left.

I will live, Brasse said to himself, sitting down at long last, his legs trembling and his hands fumbling aimlessly among the prints and papers piled in front of him. And yet he wasn't happy.

20

A LOVELY LITTLE PICTURE HAD APPEARED ON THE WALL of the studio—a photograph of a small bunch of violets. Brasse had taken it back in the summer, then retouched the print, adding colors, and fixed up a simple frame.

He had wanted to create this homage to light and life, even though it was out of season. The weather outside was freezing, but the first flakes of snow had not yet begun to fall. On the rare sunny days, the air was still and cold, or else it was blown about by a wind already full of ice.

As he hung the picture, hammering in the nail with a stone, his colleagues watched him in astonishment, as though he were making preparations to escape.

"Lovely!" they chorused, but they didn't say anything else.

He hadn't asked anyone's permission, and the photographer knew that his colleagues were waiting to see how Maltz—and, more importantly, Walter—would react. He should have sought approval, it was true, but he had simply followed his heart.

As he straightened the picture frame, his thoughts were with Baśka, his girl. That was how he thought of her. He had colored the flowers for her—as a gift. One day, he had even managed to show the picture to her. He smiled to himself at the memory.

The series of pictures of dwarfs was now complete, but over the last few weeks, Mengele had continued to send Brasse new subjects to photograph in the highest possible definition. This new wave of people, both women and men, were all ill. Baśka always managed to accompany any women who were sent. She kept the list of the prisoners to be documented and would communicate Mengele's orders about particularly interesting subjects.

After Brasse had photographed them, Wawrzyniak prepared the labels for the images. The prisoners were all suffering from a form of facial gangrene, and the neat calligraphy read *Noma faciei, cancrum oris*. Their faces were covered with enormous abscesses, which developed in the mucous membranes in the mouth and destroyed the cheeks before bursting, lacerating the facial tissue and revealing the muscles and bones of the jaw. Using the old lens, which rendered details more clearly, Brasse recorded the lesions, the devastation, and the pain.

He treated these prisoners, who looked around them with wild eyes, with a new kindness. They were all condemned to die, according to the logic of the camp, and Brasse knew that once photographed, they were no longer of any use. Mengele inflicted absurd treatments on them, pitilessly, taking no precautions, before sending them to their deaths with a quick signature on a form. Once, he even sent eight corpses to be photographed, with signs of the disease still fresh on their faces.

On one occasion when Brasse and Baśka had a brief moment to exchange a few words, she gave her opinion on the doctor's work. "Mengele thinks, as always, that there's some kind of predisposition behind this illness. But I think if he stopped to consider how malnourished these people are, he'd understand why they're ill."

His little Baśka, the graceful, brave prisoner who always smiled so warmly at him!

They never had time to say much. One day, he'd told her she was beautiful—just like that, without preamble. And she'd replied without hesitating for one second that he was beautiful too.

A few days later, they'd managed to meet.

He'd told Walter that he needed to go to Birkenau to check the identities of a few subjects he'd photographed for Mengele. Walter hadn't objected: anything for the doctor was fine by him. He hadn't even been surprised by the fact that Brasse wanted to go there urgently himself, despite the fact that the photographer hardly ever set foot outside Block 26.

That was how Brasse had managed to go and see Baśka quite openly. He'd gone into the block where she worked and found her sitting at a little desk covered in Mengele's lists. He had introduced himself to the kapo who was overseeing things and tried to look as though he had an urgent mission to accomplish. Baśka, who retained her composure throughout, looked up the names of a few prisoners he had photographed and discovered that most of them were already dead. Hardly the best circumstances in which to ingratiate himself with a girl, but they had managed to speak. The kapo left the room for a moment, and he quickly asked Baśka how she was, if she managed to sleep at night, if she had loved ones to think of. He also asked her if she was afraid, but she hadn't answered.

In a few more stolen meetings, he'd discovered more about her and told her a little about himself. At that point, they decided to stop seeing each other in that way—their meetings were already frequent enough, and there was a risk of attracting unwanted attention. The last time they'd met, in the office where Baśka worked, they had parted with a promise to invent some reason to see each other elsewhere. Before he left, he had grasped her hand. He wanted to stroke her soft, pure cheek, but he held back— somebody might have seen. So he had managed only to embrace her with his eyes. She blushed.

Several days later, they arranged to meet behind Block 20. Baśka had already let him know that she'd pass by there at a certain time, and he, covered by Brodka, had made an excuse to leave the studio for a few minutes.

He'd had the idea to bring the picture of the flowers to this rendezvous. Among all the photographs of mouths devastated by infection, he remembered this other shot, the tribute to summer that he hadn't known what to do with at the time. In a few snatched moments here and there, in great secrecy, he'd printed it and done the retouching and coloring. As he worked, he felt as if he were transmitting his warmth to her from afar. He felt an absurd sense of comfort—painful but sweet and very beautiful.

Behind Block 20, at the agreed time, he saw Baśka coming toward him. She was walking confidently, without running. Her eyes were anxious but also full of expectation and joy.

"I can't stop for long," she said.

They looked around nervously before exchanging a brief kiss. Her lips were cracked and dry. Standing close to each other in silence, they held hands for a moment, their breath mixing in white clouds condensed from the terrible cold.

"This is for you," he said, showing her the picture of the flowers.

The few violets had sprung up months earlier in the little flowerbed in front of Block 26. One SS man had wanted to destroy them immediately. It was as if the executioner were ashamed of this beauty that dared to raise its head in the midst of this hell that he had helped to construct. Others, though—men who were even more corrupt—had wanted to preserve this miracle. They were happy to see this confirmation from heaven that beauty existed even in Auschwitz and that it was there just for them, the masters of the world.

Baśka looked at the photo, then up at Brasse. Her eyes were wet with tears.

"I can't take it with me," she said. "I'm afraid they'll find it and discover that you neglected your work to print it for me."

He found himself almost offended by such prudence. If she loved him, why was her only thought for the risk they were taking? But he recognized the selfishness of his reaction. He dismissed the thought from his mind and put the photo back in his pocket.

"I'll keep it, then," he said. "I'll hang it in the laboratory, and when you come there, you'll be able to look up and see something that makes you think of life. When you do, remember that it's for you. It'll be our secret, all right?"

And now the picture was there on the wall, as promised. Everyone liked it, but no one knew yet whether this bending of the rules would be permitted.

At that moment, Walter came into the studio, clearly in a bad temper.

"What's this?" he demanded, pointing at the hanging picture.

Brasse assumed the humble and practical tone that worked best with his boss.

"I printed it myself, Herr Hauptscharführer. I wanted to test myself by trying to add a convincing touch of color to a black-and-white picture. If you don't like it, I shall destroy it immediately."

"What did you use for the color?" Walter asked, curious.

"What we have here, colored pens."

"The effect is good. Did it take you long?"

"No, it's quite a quick job."

Walter took down the picture and looked at it carefully in the cold light filtering through the window. Brasse feared he might take it away.

"Make some copies of it and color them," his boss ordered.

The photographer hadn't been expecting this, but he managed to hide his surprise.

"How many shall I make?"

"A dozen. Can I have them before tomorrow?"

"We are at your service."

The kommando printed the copies, then Brasse reluctantly put his colleagues to work coloring them following the style of his original.

Walter was pleased with the result. "Everyone at the Political Department will like them," he commented. And he took them away with a slight smile on his lips.

The next day, he gave another order.

"Brasse, print three hundred copies and color them all."

Brodka, Myszkowski, Wojcicki, Wawrzyniak, and Josefsberg—the new boy who wasn't as good at retouching as Brasse had led Walter to believe but who was nonetheless expert in printing and darkroom work—all got to work to fulfill the new demand.

One morning, Baśka came in with two women afflicted with facial gangrene. Her eyes searched the studio walls for the print of the violets, and she blushed with pleasure when she saw it hanging there. But then her gaze also fell on the hundreds of copies of the same picture, and she looked down, embarrassed.

There was simply no way Brasse could explain to her what had happened, and his powerlessness drove him to distraction.

When the portraits of the women were finished, he and Baśka said goodbye with the required formality, but this time, it seemed to him that her coldness toward him was authentic. He passed an afternoon, an evening, and a night suffering like a teenager whose girlfriend hasn't given him her usual affectionate glance.

The three hundred hand-colored postcards were nice but not perfect. The colors faded and rubbed off with the touch of a finger. Walter wanted to order three hundred more but was openly critical of the quality of this batch.

"Is there nothing we can do to fix the colors more effectively? Tell me what you think. You're the expert."

"I've thought about that, Herr Walter," Brasse replied, his answer at the ready. "The emulsion on the camera film is very good at absorbing colors made with aniline because it bonds with them and makes them indelible. If we could acquire some in sufficient quantities…"

"I see. Let me see what I can do."

Less than a week later, to everyone's great surprise, they received the colors that Brasse had requested and began working with them.

Over the next few days, Walter gradually became more good-humored than they had ever seen him before. The postcards were enormously popular among the SS officers and soldiers, and Walter was managing to sell hundreds to those who wanted to send a sentimental message from Auschwitz to their fiancées or families.

One day, Walter appeared at the studio in exceptionally high spirits. He approached Brasse, who was sitting at the photography desk, pulled some banknotes out of his pocket, and handed them to the prisoner.

"Here, Brasse. These are for you. Buy yourself something at the shop."

The notes amounted to five camp marks. The photographer looked at this small fortune for a moment and murmured his thanks.

"There'll be some for you soon," Walter said to Brodka and Myszkowski. "I know you color the postcards, and you have the right to a reward too."

The little enterprise was going well, then. Even Maltz insisted that they give him a few dozen prints and threatened to make their lives unbearable if they refused to do so. He obviously wanted to sell them to his colleagues.

Winter continued its deadly course. The gas chambers were working flat out, and trainloads of new deportees arrived nearly every day. The camp was a well-oiled machine of death. Even the typhus epidemic had been contained.

"All clear," Walter announced one day with a slight spring

in his step. "Once we'd rounded up those affected and registered them, we only had to eliminate them, and all danger of contagion passed."

The smell of burning flesh always hung over the camp, especially in the eyenings. People were being slaughtered by the thousands—new prisoners were arriving from all over Europe, but the camp was never overcrowded. Meanwhile, the false spring of Brasse's innocent flowers spread all around, awakening old feelings, memories, and thoughts of loved ones in the hearts of the jailers. Brasse imagined their postcards from Auschwitz, full of "Dear Greta," "My sweet Paulina," "Honored parents, I'm thinking of you and send you a kiss…" Postcards from hell carrying the colors of paradise. No problem for the censors there.

Walter's pockets filled up quickly, and his status in the eyes of his superiors shot up.

"I was certain that you were an untapped resource, Brasse. I knew I could expect the best from someone so inventive!"

The Erkennungsdienst's days were ones of hard work during this period, and the flowers took up almost all their time. Brasse couldn't find a moment to see Baśka, and she didn't come to the studio anymore, because Mengele's interest in prisoners suffering from facial gangrene had vanished abruptly. He had probably cataloged enough of them now.

While the doctor was deciding what his next experiments would involve, he himself bought two of the flower postcards. He sent one and hung the other in his laboratory, where Baśka saw it one evening. For a long while, she stood staring at it, full of sadness.

"Is there something wrong, Fräulein Stefańska?"

"No, nothing."

"Don't you like the flowers?"

"Yes, I like them very much."

"Would you like me to give you one of the postcards?"

"No, thank you, Herr Mengele. I'll look at yours, hanging here."

"All right. Sit down. I want to tell you something."

Baśka took a seat, restrained and impassive once more.

"I'm going away in a few days," Mengele began to explain. "I'm going to another camp for a short while. It's a temporary absence—my research here is too important to be abandoned altogether. I want you to look after the list of prisoners that I've identified to be part of my experiments. I've already given detailed instructions, and I want you to do this for me: make sure that when I return, the subjects I'm interested in are still at my disposal. Is that clear?"

"Yes, that's clear."

Silence.

"But you really don't like those flowers," he pressed. "Why do you keep looking at them like that?"

"I'm sorry..."

"No, don't worry. I'll take them down. Goodbye, Fräulein Stefańska. And thank you for your help."

"Elena Morawa!"

"Here!"

The voice of a terrified, distressed woman who was trying to sound ready and full of energy came to Brasse and Brodka from out of the darkness of the crowded barracks building. They were waiting at the entrance with their backs to the weak sun, not wanting to go in for fear that their curious gazes would offend the women inside. They also didn't want to be suffocated by the foul smell that filled the building. They had managed to convince the kapo to send the women to be photographed outside, assuring her that the pictures would be taken with the Contax straightaway, just outside the door.

"Hurry up!" the kapo yelled into the darkness.

Elena advanced from the shadows into the sunlight, shielding her eyes.

Brasse guessed the woman must be around fifty, but perhaps she was only thirty and in a few short months here had aged another twenty years from hunger and fear. He tried to encourage her with a smile, hoping that the sight of two prisoners like herself might be reassuring. They weren't calling her to be killed—at least not yet.

The woman walked with her arms wrapped around her sunken chest, trembling, and as the sunlight fell on her, it revealed the signs of her suffering. Now that he could see her better, it was clear to Brasse how weak she was, and he couldn't help thinking that it was only her special physical characteristic that was keeping her out of the gas chamber. Now that he was about to document her by taking her photograph, she would be done for.

"Hello, Elena," he said. "Come outside. Don't be afraid."

She obeyed, taking another step forward and running her hand through her hair instinctively, as though to tidy it up for these two young strangers.

"Good. Now look up toward the light," Brasse directed her. "Yes, that's it."

Lit up by the sun, Elena's eyes were the most fully alive thing about her. They were just as Hauptsturmführer Eduard Wirths, the chief medical officer, had said they would be: one blue and one brown.

Brasse and Brodka took three photos from different angles,

keeping the pupils in the center of the picture, and then took a quick portrait.

"There. All done."

Elena's face framed a question: what now?

For some reason, Brasse didn't hold back.

"Wait for more instructions," he told her. "Your eyes are special, and Dr. Wirths wants to study them in detail."

She grasped this thread of hope, nodding without smiling, already thinking of her future: could she survive until tomorrow, until next week, until liberation came? Then she turned and rejoined the other women in the cold, stinking darkness. Brasse and Brodka glimpsed the looks of amazement from her companions, who had just said goodbye to her for what they thought was the last time. There were also some envious glances.

"There aren't any more in here," the kapo announced, running her eyes down the list. "Go to Block 17."

The sun was still weak, and there was a slight wind, no longer wintry but not yet springlike. Brasse and Brodka took back the list and went on their way. On it were the names of eight women with different-colored eyes. Almost all of them were Polish, they noticed.

They were hoping to finish their work by that evening; earlier that day, the camp authorities had announced that all the female prisoners were confined to their barracks without explaining why. Brasse and Brodka were encouraged by how quickly they'd managed to photograph the first prisoner; they'd be back in Block

26 before long. This job was less difficult than photographing men and women with facial gangrene, but their experiences over the last few months had destroyed any illusions they might have had about the outcome of this research: to smile at those involved and to reassure them was to lie. Mengele might have been away from the camp, but the experiments were continuing. There were plenty of other doctors who were now free to invent any field of study they liked.

Brasse and Brodka carried on. The other women were in no better state than Elena had been, and all were frightened to death at being called outside. But their eyes were magical, disturbing, mysterious.

As he took the fourth portrait, Brasse's thoughts turned to Baśka. They saw each other less now that she was once again a prisoner just like any other.

If she had different colored eyes, she would be lost, he thought. In Auschwitz, being special could mean salvation, or it could mean an even worse death. Whatever happened, though, these women would always be preserved in these photographs: unique, special. *As we all are,* he thought to himself. A portrait, if done carefully, always revealed this: the precious individuality we all contain.

This thought decided him: he would take a portrait of Baśka, and it had to be the best portrait he had ever made.

Soon afterward, running the risk of being discovered, Brasse bribed a female kapo who seemed a little less cold than the others.

"What do you want?" she asked, staring at the unexpected bounty of a few camp marks.

"I want you to take a message to a prisoner. She's a relative of mine—Baśka Tytoniak."

"Baśka. Yes, I know her. So?"

"Tell her that Brasse, the photographer, needs to see her about an urgent matter. She was Dr. Mengele's secretary, and she brought prisoners to the studio to be photographed for him. She'll find a way of coming. Tell her to come to the Identification Service today, no later than two o'clock."

He'd be able to use the sunlight.

"Is that clear?"

The woman leered at him. "Will you two be alone at two o'clock? Is that what you want?"

"That's none of your business."

"Oh yes, it is. Have you got any others like her?"

He didn't insist and passed her another banknote. The postcards were still selling well, and soon he'd be getting more money.

Later, in Block 26, he acted as though everything were normal. His colleagues were busy coloring flowers. Walter had all but stopped any other work, and he only dropped in occasionally to collect the merchandise.

Brasse's heart was beating madly. Today, he would have the chance to photograph the object of his affection. If he was discovered using the studio for personal reasons, his superiors would probably tolerate it, so it wasn't fear that was making his heart beat at a quickened pace: he felt like a lover getting ready for a first meeting. He and Baśka had seen each other several times—they'd talked and even kissed. But today, he feared being rejected by her or finding out that he might have asked too much.

She arrived at the studio at half past one, alone. She looked at him as though expecting terrible news.

"Welcome," he greeted her.

The other members of the kommando looked at him indulgently. There were no secrets between them.

"What's going on?" Baśka asked. "Why did you ask me to come?"

"Sit down," he answered, pointing to the revolving chair. "I want to take your portrait."

His words only served to increase her fear.

"Why?" she demanded, almost shouting. "What for?"

Brasse moved toward her and tried to put his arms around her, which made things even worse.

"Have you got something to tell me?" she cried. "Am I about to die?"

"No, no."

"Don't lie to me! Not you!"

"Baśka..."

"It's too dangerous."

"No, no, don't be scared. We'll do it quickly. I want to have your portrait. I'll keep it a secret, just for me."

He held her close, and the other men looked on in bewilderment.

"Hurry up," said Wawrzyniak.

"Yes, get on with it," urged Brodka, and he began to arrange the lights.

Their familiarity and friendliness helped calm Baśka down.

But Brasse wanted to do it all himself, and he made his colleagues leave the room. He sat her down and walked around her, adjusted the lamps, opened the window and then closed it again, and perfected her pose with gentle but firm touches of his hands.

She let him work but was still sitting rather stiffly.

When he looked at her through the viewfinder, he could sense her discomfort, so he went back over to her and took her hand.

"My love, I want this photograph. I want it for me and for you. I want to show you how beautiful you are. I want you to see yourself as I see you. Then you'll never doubt my feelings for you. And I want to keep you with me always, like a lover would. Don't you want that too?"

She looked at him tenderly, with something indefinable in her expression. Something to which he couldn't ascribe a name.

He took the pictures. One, two, three. They were good, even with that expression that was somewhere between trust and surrender.

"There," he said. "All done."

It was exactly what he'd said to the women with eyes of different colors.

"Don't show me to anybody else!" Baśka ordered him. "Nobody! Not even your friends."

He didn't understand. "What are you afraid of? Even if Walter found out, he'd put up with it, and much more…"

"It's not him I'm thinking of. It's me. I don't want you to show my picture to other people, like you did—" She hesitated.

"Like I did?"

"With my flowers."

He sat down and buried his face in his hands. Those beautiful flowers, those damned flowers that were being sent all over the Reich with their messages of love.

Baśka was crying now. He too wanted to weep.

"Nobody will see it," he promised. "I'll develop it and print it myself. I'll make only one copy. And I'll keep it hidden. But don't cry, please."

She dried her tears, rubbing her face with her hands. She looked like a child. Brasse felt his heart go out to her. Then, finally, she smiled. Now she was happy, or at least he hoped she was.

As she left, she embraced him and even thanked him.

But he felt that he was the one who had received a precious gift.

2 2

BRASSE WOULD NEVER FORGET THE TIME HE WAS drawn—if only for a short while—into the part of the camp thirsty not only for death but also for blood, humiliation, and despair. It was then that he felt close to succumbing to the madness that Walter had promised him.

"Hauptsturmführer Dr. Wirths is also very pleased with your work," Walter had said to him. "He's coming here today to ask you to work for him again. I fear he may want to steal you away from the Erkennungsdienst to work full time on a special project."

"I hope not, Herr Walter. I like being here."

"You don't need to tell me that, Brasse. I know that you feel safe here. But the Reich's needs come before personal safety. We have duties, and we will fulfill them. Our medical branch is in the middle of important scientific experiments, and you must consider yourself at their service. I will, however, do my best to ensure that they don't transfer you to that team permanently."

Brasse had nodded gratefully but was still perplexed.

"Don't fret about it," Walter had said. "Carry on work as normal. When Dr. Wirths arrives, I'll bring him over here personally, so it will be clear that what you're doing for them is only possible thanks to my approval."

But when the two SS men came into the laboratory together an hour later, it was Wirths who gave the orders.

"Over the next few weeks, you will document gynecological experiments in Block 10, overseen by Dr. Clauberg," he told Brasse.

"What...must I do?"

"I'll send a group of female Jewish prisoners. You must photograph them for cataloging purposes. Then you will receive instructions on how to photograph the experiments themselves. The women will be accompanied by a medical expert, Dr. Maximilian Samuel. Follow his instructions."

Everyone knew who Dr. Clauberg was. He was often seen around camp in civilian clothes and had the gentle manner of a family doctor. The only thing they knew about Dr. Samuel was that he was a prisoner, just like them. Or perhaps not.

"They're studying sterilization methods," Walter had explained to him. "That's all I know. It's research that will help to solve once and for all the problem of inferior races reproducing."

He'd said it just like that, as though it was something that Brasse was obviously already aware of and in agreement with. Had he served the Germans too effectively? Did they think he felt himself to be not only their servant but also someone who actually wanted to be involved in their projects?

He'd asked himself these questions in the hours before the group of women arrived. Instead of finding answers, he felt only a sense of immense anguish growing inside him: it was as though he were shut in a dark trap and couldn't breathe. He'd wanted to escape but had pushed the feeling away, telling himself that it couldn't be worse than any of the other times. It would just be yet another group of prisoners to photograph before they were sentenced to death.

And now here he was. And his eyes saw.

Before him, Dr. Samuel was holding a pair of spoon-shaped forceps. He brought them up close to the vagina of a seventeen- or eighteen-year-old girl who was heavily sedated, having been given a narcotic injection. The two women who had brought the group of girls over to the studio—and who had positioned this girl on the gyneco-logical examination chair with her legs open—watched impassively. The doctor pushed the forceps inside her—slowly, gently, but unhesi-tatingly. Two minutes later, he delicately extracted the young woman's uterus through her vagina and deposited it in a basin.

"Come closer, Herr Brasse. I'll show you the details we want to be particularly visible in your photos."

Brasse moved forward numbly. He couldn't keep his eyes off the bleeding organ, tormented by the sight of the unconscious woman's violated uterus. He wanted to say something but couldn't. He felt the dizziness rising up inside him and a feeling of ever-increasing nausea that grew and grew and couldn't be overcome.

"Here, look at the veins with the whitish coloring," Dr. Samuel encouraged. "That's the effect of the drugs that we administered to the patient. That's what we're especially interested in. Understood?"

The veins, the white stripes, the girl's white skin that was taking on an even whiter, unbearable pallor as a result of the pool of blood spreading between her legs. And the smell of that blood…

"Understood?" Samuel repeated. "Are you listening to me?"

"Yes…"

"Right. Take the photos."

Brasse tried to focus. There was nothing else he could do.

He did as he was told.

Then they covered the girl and hauled her out of the room.

They brought in another girl, and another, who all submitted to the injection without resisting. He couldn't understand why. Had they already been through worse things? Had they been promised that nothing terrible would happen to them?

He watched the procedures and took the pictures, as he'd been instructed. The glare of the lamps, positioned with great care as always, had never seemed so violent to him. He began to long for darkness, for the night and for silence. He felt dirty, polluted by a stain that he would never be able to wash away.

There were five girls in total. It was all over within the space of an hour.

But that was only the beginning.

That evening, when the photographs had been developed and printed, the images of the five girls' extracted organs all looked the same.

"These black-and-white photographs are next to useless to our doctors," Dr. Clauberg, who was leading the research, complained to Walter the following day.

"We need color photographs," Walter told Brasse in turn.

Brasse didn't reply. He only spread his hands in a gesture of powerlessness.

"I'll get some color film in Katowice," Walter concluded. "Don't take any more pictures like this until I've got the right materials."

He made as if to leave, but Brasse called him back.

"Herr Walter."

"Yes."

"We won't be able to develop the color photographs here. We haven't got the right equipment, as you know. We'll have to send them elsewhere…"

"Of course, Herr Brasse. Stop telling me things I know very well!"

So even though Brasse continued to take more of these kinds of photographs, he never saw the color negatives. It was a small relief.

Over the next few days, Brasse tried to avoid madness by thinking about Baśka, but the thought of her and what could happen to her, too, only worsened his growing anxiety. He couldn't sleep at night.

It was as though the walls of his den had crumbled, and he found himself staring death in the face, prey to a pack of ferocious dogs. The girls from the hysterectomies appeared before his eyes again, mute and resigned.

He'd found out that the first group of patients had been Greek Jews. He imagined their journey from Greece to Auschwitz, from the sunshine and artistic glories of that mythical country to this godforsaken place. He tried to comfort himself by clinging to the slightest illusion. Dr. Samuel had assured him that the operation did not usually carry with it any damaging consequences, but Brasse knew full well that after the operation and the photographs, all that awaited those girls was death.

"These women could survive the trauma," the doctor had said in a professional tone. "That's why Dr. Clauberg feels it might be possible to launch a real campaign of complete sterilization."

At night, the girls' eyes, the mechanical nature of the medical procedure, the color of the blood, the pulse of life that still moved the organs being photographed, the indifference of the women who assisted the doctor—all this merged into one nightmare vision for Brasse. To escape it and the feelings that ate away at him, he would have liked to close his eyes and then, behind his closed eyelids, close his eyes yet again. But he couldn't.

This happened in Block 26, in my studio, he kept telling himself. *I've been here more than three years, and I've managed to see as little as possible. And now they've come to me, and they're doing these things in front of me. And I can't do anything…*

And what of Baśka? They had lost contact recently. He didn't even know what work had been assigned to her now that Mengele was away. He hadn't been able to show her the portrait yet, and at night, he would imagine the joy that this act of love would bring her. It was the only way he could fall asleep. Yet every morning, he would open his eyes again and return immediately to horror and blood.

"The progress of science never pauses," announced Walter one day in his office. "Soon we will also photograph experiments being undertaken by Dr. Johann Paul Kremer."

Brasse couldn't withhold a shiver of disgust.

"What is it, Herr Brasse? Don't you like the sight of blood?"

"No, Herr Hauptscharführer, I—"

"Didn't you once want to go to war? Unless I'm mistaken, you were captured while trying to cross the border into Slovakia to join the Polish army in France. Isn't that right?"

Why couldn't he let it drop?

"Answer me. Isn't that right?"

"Yes."

"You'd have seen much worse things in war, you know. Have you ever seen amputations, open wounds, heads pierced by grenade fragments?"

"No."

"That is death, Herr Brasse, and it doesn't ask anyone's permission. Here we're simply conducting medical research, with all suitable precautions. And it's research for the benefit of humanity. Do you realize that?"

Brasse didn't move. He kept his eyes fixed in front of him. He couldn't reply without compromising himself.

"Do you mean to defy me, Herr Brasse?" Walter thundered.

"No, sir."

"Are you under the illusion that you're indispensable to us and therefore safe from our anger?"

"No, I'm not under any illusion. I do my job, Herr Hauptscharführer, as I always have."

Walter studied Brasse's face in silence for a long time, his eyes full of suspicion.

"I can't see inside your head, my dear photographer, so I am obliged to judge you by your actions. And these, I admit, are beyond reproach. Carry on doing what you are doing, and keep your ideas to yourself."

Brasse didn't dare reply that he hadn't tried to express his ideas. It was his soul that Walter wanted, and Brasse was more than willing to keep that to himself.

"Still, you needn't worry," his boss concluded. "Professor Kremer doesn't do gynecological research. He studies organ failure in subjects who've undergone long periods of starvation. As I understand it, you'll see only autopsies of Jews who've just been liquidated, and you'll be asked to photograph their livers in particular. Is that clear?"

"Will the autopsies be carried out...here?"

"Yes. The weakest prisoners will be carried here, and you will photograph them. Then they will be killed by lethal injection and immediately dissected by medical experts. Their livers must be analyzed immediately, as soon as the vital functions cease. If you want to know more, ask the doctors carrying out the autopsies—they're Polish. Any more questions?"

Walter was furious. He had clearly taken Brasse's none-too-discreet suggestion that the autopsies shouldn't take place in Block 26 as a personal insult, a veiled suggestion that Walter had surrendered to the demands of his SS colleagues. Or perhaps, even worse, he had interpreted it as an allusion to the fact that their ready availability was something he turned to his own advantage.

"Get out, Brasse. Get out before I begin to suspect that you no longer have the required energy to serve our cause."

Brasse did as he was told, but instead of taking the shortest route back to Block 26, he wandered around, allowing his eyes to take in scenes of camp life: work teams urged on by shouts and blows; ill and weak prisoners who hadn't managed to go to work and who looked around them in terror at the idea that they might already have been put on the wrong list; a cart full of corpses collected by a work team being taken to the crematorium. From a distance, an SS official saw him and recognized him as the photographer who had taken an excellent portrait of him in his new uniform. He'd had two copies made to send home to his father, who must surely be very proud of him.

"Hello, Herr Brasse. Are you looking to photograph someone? I'm afraid you won't find many good subjects here."

Brasse smiled weakly but didn't reply. He must have looked like a fool, or like someone who'd been wandering in a forest for a long time and had lost his path, his strength, and even the memory of where he'd been going.

The SS man approached him with kindness, even concern. "Are you all right?"

"I— Excuse me," Brasse stammered. "I need to go to Birkenau to receive instructions for photographs of—of some prisoners."

"Birkenau's that way."

Brasse looked down, intimidated, like a child caught stealing from the kitchen.

"Of course, that way. Thank you, Herr Obersturmführer."

But he couldn't pluck up the courage to make his way there, to go and look for Baśka. *She might already be dead*, he told himself. And he only had a photograph of her. The only beautiful picture he'd taken for weeks.

23

"Oh, that one? She was pretty, very pretty. She's dead."

"Dead?"

"Yes, she poisoned herself. She couldn't stand it anymore. And she was so beautiful!"

The prisoner, who worked in the crematorium, was happy to be able to smoke a cigarette and have three more hidden in his pocket. He was one of the informers Brasse was using to try to get information about Baśka. His girl had disappeared, but her name hadn't appeared on any lists of eliminated prisoners. If they'd transferred her, it must have been done without warning, and even he, with all his connections, couldn't get his hands on the latest list of transferees.

After the man had confirmed that he didn't have any news of Baśka, Brasse had tried to avoid arousing suspicion by asking about other women. This man was telling him now about a girl Brasse remembered all too well, who hadn't gone unnoticed in the camp.

"Did you know her?" he asked, registering Brasse's surprise.

The prisoner, who enjoyed passing on sensational information, was pleased by this reaction to the news of the suicide.

Brasse shook himself. "I took her portrait," he replied reluctantly. "A couple of weeks ago."

"A portrait?"

"Yes, she wanted me to. She told me it was for her mother. She came to Block 26. She looked elegant, her uniform was all clean and ironed, and she'd put her hair up. She had a wonderful figure, and with her hair done, you could see her neck and her lovely face. A real picture."

Brasse remembered every detail, but he struggled to voice the words, as though suddenly his image of her had shattered and he were trying to piece it together again. He couldn't believe that this young SS auxiliary, who'd been in charge of the Radio Service in the commandant's office, had killed herself.

"Even though she was working for them, she must have been sensitive as well as beautiful," the prisoner said. "Too beautiful. I used to see her sometimes, standing at the window of her office for ages. You can see the entrance to the crematorium ovens from there. For the whole of her shift, she must have watched carts full of naked corpses going past, then she'd see them come out empty, and all that was left of the bodies was smoke going up into the sky, impossible to ignore. She couldn't bear it. She had a soul, you see."

Brasse smiled at this. "Yes, she had a soul," he agreed.

A tormented soul. He knew that very well.

He didn't tell the prisoner what he'd done for the beautiful German auxiliary. He decided to keep it to himself.

She'd arrived at the Identification Service one sunny morning, graceful and enchanting. She looked like a little goddess. Brasse and his colleagues had welcomed her with much gallant solicitude, even though they had to treat her with the utmost respect, as she wore a uniform bearing the same colors as the SS uniforms.

Auxiliary workers didn't usually have any contact with prisoners, but she didn't seem to care about making an exception.

"Are you Herr Brasse?" she'd asked the photographer.

She'd heard about him—his fame as a portraitist had spread among the camp officials.

"I want you to take my portrait. You and nobody else. Do you understand?"

Brasse nodded, signaling to Brodka to leave the laboratory. Brodka obeyed, slightly offended and very curious.

"All right," he said. "Sit down here."

As he pointed to the revolving chair, he noticed the slight scent of perfume in the air. It was sweet and delicate, and it went to his head as though he'd been slapped in the face.

The young woman sat down and smoothed her skirt. Her

ankles emerged beneath it, perfectly formed, as did her little feet in shiny shoes. Everything about her spoke of order—of the city, of normal life.

As he arranged the lamps and continued to catch the scent of perfume, he felt her watching him. In a flash, he was transported back to a vision of the past. Himself, young, twenty years old, broad shouldered, wearing a new suit, with a bit of money to spend thanks to his work in his uncle's studio. Himself in a bar with other young men and women, making the girls laugh, drawing attention to himself, saying the right things to flatter them, make them blush, suggest an intimacy full of promise. He'd never been a real ladies' man—hadn't had the time or inclination—but girls liked him, and he knew it. These were recollections from another world, a thousand years ago, and the memory of them went through him in an explosion of burning nostalgia.

The auxiliary's voice was very soft. "I want a nice portrait to send to my mother."

Brasse had his back to her, and before turning around to look at her, he closed his eyes tight, reminding himself to remain serious and impassive.

"A nice portrait—of course. Now, don't look directly at the camera. Turn away slightly, like that," he said, positioning her.

She remained impassive, like a queen. "I want my mother to see how I am—that I'm still myself, that I'm beautiful."

Brasse talked to her just as he would an important client entering his studio in town. "You'll be happy with the result, trust me."

"Because I am beautiful, aren't I? What do you think?"

She was staring at him almost anxiously, waiting for his reply. She'd shifted her pose to ask him this question, but he didn't react.

"Beautiful, Fräulein, yes."

"And am I beautiful in this uniform?"

He tried to maintain a professional tone. "The uniform…is very neat and suits you well."

"And what if I took it off? I'd be more myself, don't you think?"

"Well…"

She came to a sudden decision and began to unbutton her jacket. Brasse stood still, stunned, watching her.

"Do you know what I really want?"

The jacket fell to the ground, and she began to unbutton her shirt. Soon he could see her lace bra, clinging to her full, soft breasts.

"Fräulein…"

"Go on. Don't be afraid. I want a topless photograph—that's why I wanted everyone else to leave the room. Can you do it? Is it against the rules? You'll only show it to me, won't you?"

"Yes…of course."

She dropped her bra on top of her shirt, which she'd left on the desk. Brasse tried to pull himself together, concentrating more intensely than he'd ever done since arriving at the camp. But when he turned to look at the young woman with as much professional detachment as he could muster, he was still taken aback.

She was sitting with her chest thrown forward, shoulders

back, hands gripping the chair and arms tensed against her sides, showing off her breasts. And they were splendid: firm and perfectly formed, the nipples seemingly suspended in the air. Her skin was pale, almost lunar, and translucent. A blue vein was just visible between her neck and her breasts, and this disturbed him more than anything else. Her face was perfectly white too—its features clear and unlined, animated by an unnerving determination. He noticed that she'd put on a touch of lipstick before coming, which made her lips stand out amid all the whiteness.

He tried to tear his eyes away from this enchantment, thinking that one of his superiors could come in at any moment. It would be disastrous—for him but especially for her. He took the pictures swiftly. As the young woman got dressed again, calm under his hungry gaze, Brasse was both relieved and distraught at the same time.

"When will they be ready?" she asked.

"By tomorrow, Fräulein."

"I can't come tomorrow. I'll come back in a few days. Can I rely on your discretion?"

"Yes, of course."

When she was dressed, her uniform once again covered her perfectly, like impenetrable armor. She went out with her head held high, to the admiring glances of the prisoners.

Brasse left the studio, still dazed. His companions teased him. There usually wasn't much to joke about, but when the chance presented itself, laughter was a welcome release.

As promised, Brasse developed and printed the compromising pictures himself, and he couldn't suppress a feeling of excitement as he did so.

Three days later, she came back to the studio, as neat and as elegant as ever.

"Very good," she commented, inspecting the portraits.

The two of them were alone again, not wanting anyone to see the photographs.

"Are they really for your mother?" he dared ask.

She remained calm. "Don't worry. They really are."

She was about to leave, and Brasse longed to be able to hold her back, to speak to her more.

"Take the negatives with you. That way, you'll have everything, and nobody will ever be able to make copies," he suggested.

She glanced at him, and this time, there was a hint of mischief in her eyes.

"No, you keep them, Herr Brasse. Keep them safe. I'm worried that I'd be the one who'd do the wrong thing with them."

He agreed, not suspecting anything.

He hadn't seen her again, and two weeks had passed.

Now she was dead. Had she already decided to kill herself, the day she came to him? Brasse thought about this for a long time after he'd said goodbye to the prisoner who'd given him the news. Then he told himself that yes, she must already have wanted to end it all.

And he hadn't seen that at the time.

He tried to find a reason for her action, pondering it for longer than he did any of the other things that happened in the camp. She had probably sent the pictures of her untamed beauty to someone. To her mother, as she'd said? Who could say? In the end, he came to see what she'd done as an extreme protest against the violence of every gesture, every bureaucratic action, every formal salute that occurred in this place of madness. A protest expressed not with words but with her own body.

The prisoner who'd given Brasse the news—who, for hours and hours each day, loaded corpses into the crematorium ovens—had been right: she couldn't possibly bear the spectacle that she saw every day through her window.

And now she was just another memory of Auschwitz, another crazed memory to be put out of his mind.

He thought of the negatives that he'd hidden as well as he could. They still existed and must never fall into the wrong hands. He felt as if he were guarding the woman herself—that mysterious servant of the enemy of mankind who, in the midst of the inferno, had simply wanted to assert her existence as a woman.

It occurred to him that one day, thanks to these negatives, he might be able to pay tribute to her. He could give them to her mother, her father, or her lover. And in handing them over, he would be able to tell the story of an isolated, desperate young woman whom history had pushed to the edge of a yawning abyss.

The photographs he'd been taking every day for years contained the memory of all the people involved: prisoners, prison guards, corrupt and twisted doctors. He was fast becoming the custodian of these images. They were all cataloged in his archive, placed in their correct groups—victors and oppressors with other victors and oppressors, victims with other victims—but the German girl, full of innocent, lively beauty, had wanted to stand apart from all of them in her own category.

These thoughts carried into the future, forging a link between his own destiny and that of the photographs. They could give some kind of meaning to his own survival; protecting this memorial would give him a focus for the years to come. And that focus might help him from descending into madness. He thought of a thousand faces, eyes, and stories. He must have photographed at least fifty thousand prisoners and hundreds of Nazi officials. He thought, too, of the picture of Baśka. He still didn't even know if she was alive or dead—all he had of her was the portrait.

One evening during roll call, somebody shouted out his name.

"Photographer Brasse from the Identification Service, report immediately!"

He stepped forward, fearing something terrible, as always.

The other prisoners dispersed, and an officer came over to him with a quizzical look in his eyes.

"I am Hauptsturmführer Heinrich Schwarz. Are you Brasse?"

"Yes, sir," he answered in German. "Prisoner 3444 reporting as ordered!"

Answering in the officers' native tongue usually helped to

make them more well disposed toward him, but Schwarz had a very precise mission and was not to be influenced.

"I'm conducting an investigation for the camp commandants, and I expect your full collaboration. If you don't cooperate, you'll be sent straight to your death. Do you understand?"

"Yes, sir."

"Did you recently take a photograph in the Identification Service studio of one of the female auxiliaries from the Radio Service? A young blond woman who arrived in uniform but wanted photographs…in nonregulation poses?"

Brasse didn't hesitate. The camp officials obviously already knew everything and had seen the photographs or at least copies.

"Yes, sir. I took the photographs as she requested."

The official continued to scrutinize him. Perhaps he wanted to ask him why he had taken the liberty of photographing an Aryan woman, a worker for the Reich, seminaked…

"Have you got the negatives?"

"Yes, sir. I filed them in the Identification Service's office, as it is my duty to with all the pictures we take."

Schwarz seemed to consider delving deeper into the workings of this service but decided against it.

"Can you hand those negatives to me straightaway?"

"Certainly, sir. With your permission, I'll go and get them immediately."

"Go. I'll wait here."

Brasse hurried off, ashamed of feeling so afraid, not allowing himself to think of the young woman and her despair. He arrived at Block 26 out of breath, found the negatives quickly, and rushed back to the official, who examined them and seemed satisfied with what he saw.

"Very well, Herr Brasse. I order you not to tell anyone about this regrettable episode. I'm told that you can be counted on, and I trust the opinion of my colleagues. This woman never existed. Is that understood?"

"Yes, sir. She never existed."

He remained still, standing to attention and trying to control his breath and his racing heart as the official walked away. He realized that he didn't even know the young woman's name. It was too late to ask about her. Her beautiful picture, her protest, her cry of pain was now in the hands of Hauptsturmführer Schwarz. The Nazi would do as he wished with all that remained of her. The first thing would no doubt be to corrupt her memory and use her beauty for his own pleasure. Then, when he was done with her, he would deny that she had ever existed.

This mustn't happen anymore, Brasse said to himself, feeling invested with a new responsibility far greater than himself. He knew now what he must do and why. Perhaps he would die, but all those who had souls had to be able to see. And understand. And judge. And cry. And remember.

Was that not what photographs were for?

PART THREE

Auschwitz, 1944–45: Rebellion and Testimony

2 4

"Please sit down, Herr Brasse."

The photographer hesitated before he took his seat and didn't relax in his chair. He was on edge and couldn't help looking at the floor.

"Come now. Despite what you may have heard, I don't eat people."

Hauptsturmführer Hans Aumeier looked at Brasse with satisfaction. He was enjoying the effect that his reputation for cruelty and sadism was having on the well-built young Polish man who sat in front of him, waiting to know his fate.

"Whenever I see you at work in the Erkennungsdienst, you're always more at ease. That's your lair, isn't it?"

"It's…my kommando, sir."

"Of course. And you do excellent work there. Everyone says so. And I've seen with my own eyes how your colleagues obey you: how quickly they follow your instructions, how trustingly they turn to you for advice. Even Hauptscharführer Walter seems to hang on your every word."

Brasse felt lost. Aumeier had come into Block 26 increasingly often over the last few days. He always seemed relaxed, even friendly. He would smoke a cigarette with Walter, and they would laugh and joke together. Aumeier would ask the kommando intelligent questions as they retouched a picture or assessed a print in the light of day. But Brasse was on his guard. It was clear that these breaks from work in the Political Department weren't just for fun. Aumeier was observing everything. He acted as though he had come seeking amusement, but in fact, he behaved as if he were seeking to confirm a suspicion. Something about the composure of their little group obviously irritated him.

"Isn't that so?" Aumeier pressed. "Answer me. You speak and understand German very well."

"I obey orders, Herr Hauptsturmführer, and our superior officer knows how to get the best out of us."

Aumeier stiffened, but his tone remained polite.

"No, Herr Brasse, don't play games with me. I think you're the one who knows how to get the best out of others, wherever you are. But don't worry. I haven't called you here to reprimand you. On the contrary, I've brought you here to tell you that in our eyes, your authority makes you a precious commodity."

Brasse's face was impassive, but his mind was working furiously. What was going on? Were they going to give him a promotion?

Aumeier smiled broadly, and his gaze was friendly, as though he were already enjoying the effect of the words he was about to say.

"Tell me, Herr Brasse, what would you do if we were to set you free? Don't you want to see your family again? Your mother, your brothers?"

What did this monster know about his family?

"I...hope they are well," he managed.

"I hope so too, Herr Brasse. But you could find out for yourself. Wouldn't you like to?"

Home. Brasse's heart began to beat wildly, but he realized he wasn't actually relieved in any way. His mind knew what his soul still denied: there was only one way of getting out of Auschwitz.

Aumeier showed him a piece of paper bearing the official stamp of the Reich's Population Office.

"You know very well that you could leave straightaway. Sign this recognition that you belong to the German race, and I guarantee that before beginning to serve in the Wehrmacht, as is your duty, you will be allowed to spend two weeks at home in Żywiec. Your mother would be happy, don't you think?"

Brasse remained silent, not knowing what to say.

The officer sighed but didn't lose his cool.

"Come now, Brasse. You are German, as we know very well. Your insistence on declaring yourself to be Polish has already earned you more than three years' internment. You have made yourself very useful, I admit, and you are in fact already serving our cause, but we can't ignore your true nature. That is the reason we're fighting this war: so that each race can play the role assigned to it by God.

"By denying that you are German, even though your grandfather and father were German, you are denying this basic truth. And I can't accept that, each day, Germany's finest sons should die in the hundreds on the Russian front, fighting the Bolsheviks just as your father did, while you are here taking pictures in a cozy studio."

A long silence followed. Brasse couldn't think straight, but he had to say something.

"Herr…"

"Don't speak to me in German, Brasse!" Aumeier thundered. "Don't speak to me in German unless you mean to serve your race!" The officer got to his feet, struggling to contain his anger. "Your mother may be Polish, but still, don't you think she'd be pleased to see you?"

These continual references to his mother, as though Aumeier knew her, worried Brasse. But he mustn't panic.

"Herr Hauptsturmführer, I'm here precisely because I disobeyed my mother and tried to escape from Poland. She wanted me to stay there and prepare to serve. I wasn't a good son, and perhaps she, more than anyone else, has given up hope of me changing my mind."

Aumeier was now standing behind him, contemplating what to do. Brasse even thought he heard him grinding his teeth, and he was relieved when the officer began to speak again.

"In order to make the most of your talents, we need to convince you to join us, not force you. I understand this. We are now close to victory, and the army needs stronger forces. You could still distinguish yourself, Brasse. You could have an excellent career. Here, as you know, the only success possible is to survive until we decide that you're managing too well. Do you still want to live this way?"

Brasse nodded.

Aumeier sat down again and stared at the photographer as though confronted by some inexplicable phenomenon.

"Look at me."

Brasse obeyed.

There was an iron resolve, an absolute determination, in the German's eyes. Brasse thought briefly how interesting it would have been to capture on film this very look, with all its energy. It would have made a wonderful photograph.

"What is the point of what you're doing, Herr Brasse? You cling to your conviction of being Polish, even to the point of risking your own life. There is something I admire in that. But where will this obstinacy get you? We are using you, and you are serving us well. You are helping us to preserve an ordered record of our work. But now you can do more. You can change your fate!"

Brasse held the officer's gaze. This man might believe himself to be omnipotent, but he couldn't read Brasse's mind. Changing his fate was precisely what had been on Brasse's mind for weeks now.

"I'll give it some thought, Herr Hauptsturmführer," he said. "But in the meantime, please let me return to the work that, as you say, I can do—and wish to do—well."

Aumeier was furious now. Brasse focused on not allowing his fear to show. One wrong word and he'd be dead by the evening.

"Other Polish men—especially Silesians like you—have accepted, you know," the officer spat. "Now they are free and are proud to wear the SS uniform."

"Yes, I know," replied Brasse evenly.

"Do you regret that?"

"No, I respect them."

He knew all about the Poles who had enlisted in the German special forces. One morning a few weeks earlier, four young SS men had come into Block 26, and he had, as usual, addressed them in perfect German.

"How may I help you?"

He'd been amazed to hear one of them reply in bad German.

"I don't understand…"

"What language would you like to speak?" he asked.

"You're Polish, aren't you?" said one of the soldiers. "Let's speak Polish."

Yes, they were Polish. And they were SS.

He hadn't been able to hold his tongue.

"But…which part of Poland are you from?"

So it was that he'd discovered that they were from the Tatra mountains, near Zakopane. The most educated of them explained, with a hint of pride, how they'd come to be where they were.

"Our province is on the Slovakian border, but the Germans see us as being theirs because we're part of Galicia. You know, the old Kingdom of Galicia in the northern part of the Austrian Empire. Anyway, it worked out well for us. They treat us as their equals."

"And you enlisted voluntarily?"

"I did, yes," said one of the men.

"I didn't want to, but what else could I do?" admitted another.

They were perfectly calm—they considered themselves lucky, and it showed. All sorts of questions had sprung to Brasse's mind: Had they already killed? Had they tortured anyone? Had they denied a piece of bread or a word of comfort to one of their compatriots? Had they already tricked a Polish child, a Jewish child, or a Romani child, by lying to them about the nearby gas chambers?

But he didn't want to think about them now as he continued his conversation with Aumeier. He didn't want to think about the sadness he'd felt seeing their naive smiles and the absurd belief they had that they were lucky because they were on the winning side. He couldn't understand how his own countrymen could give in like that. However, he also knew that he held a privileged position in the camp, so he was in no position to judge them.

Aumeier pressed him further.

"You respect them, do you? No, Herr Brasse. Your own refusal is itself a condemnation of their acceptance. And we cannot tolerate this attitude. You've met Poles who have joined our ranks. You've taken photographs of them for their identity documents, haven't you?"

"Yes."

"And you spoke to them?"

"Yes."

"And you didn't try to dissuade them? Or at least you made your disapproval clear?"

"No, Herr Hauptsturmführer. You can ask them if you like. I didn't express any opinion about their choices. In fact, it was they who looked at me as though my own choice were the wrong one."

Aumeier relaxed somewhat. He seemed to be considering his next move. Brasse was trying to avoid another attack—he'd made his decision, and there was no more to be said. His conscience hadn't changed since that day long ago in 1940 when, still free, he had refused to sign documents certifying his membership of the German race. Just as it had been then, his mind was made up, and they could do what they liked with him. He felt exhausted, tired of this state of suspense. He wanted to escape from the uncertainty; if he must die, he wanted it to be straightaway.

"May I go?" He surprised himself with the urgent, almost irritated tone in which he asked the question.

Aumeier eyed him resentfully.

"Yes, Herr Brasse, you may go. But from now on, you are in danger. Don't forget that. Some of my colleagues are still protecting you, but in my eyes, you're a traitor, and sooner or later, you will suffer the consequences. Do you understand?"

"Yes, sir, I understand."

"Now go, before I change my mind."

Brasse saluted and took a step backward toward the door.

"One last thing, Herr Brasse."

"Sir?"

"Hauptscharführer Walter and his assistant, Hofmann, have received new orders from me about your work. I want you to know that I'm the one who will decide how much you learn about those orders."

"Yes, sir."

Brasse made his way outside, his legs shaking. The sun was low, its light blinding, and he turned toward its splendor. He let the cold light of the morning fall on his face and filled his lungs with chilly air. Then he squared his shoulders. He felt himself to be a man. Perhaps this sun was announcing the last spring of his life. However, his body stubbornly repeated that it was still something to have gotten through a fourth winter in Auschwitz, despite continuing obstinately with his one act of heroism: his determined attachment to his country.

He went back to Block 26 with the image of his mother vivid in his mind, but he managed, bit by bit, to push it into a part of his brain that he always kept firmly closed off.

He found Hofmann waiting for him in the laboratory.

"Brasse," he said. "From today, you won't be photographing any more Poles. There's no point wasting resources on those shits."

The photographer didn't reply. Hofmann's desire to offend him was too obvious. The *P* sewn into the triangle on his uniform made his nationality clear to the SS man, if he didn't know it already.

"We stopped photographing Jews, now we're dropping Poles too," Hofmann continued. "From now on, you'll photograph only Germans, and also Slovaks and Slovenians because their governments are collaborating with the Reich. Is that clear?"

It was. Just as it had been clear that when they stopped photographing Jews, it was because most of them were being sent directly to the gas chambers, with no time being wasted in deciding their fate.

"Is there a problem?"

Did Hofmann want to hear Brasse protest in defense of his compatriots? Or did he want to see him breathe a sigh of relief at the thought that he himself was only half Polish?

"No, Herr Hofmann. I understand."

He kept his comments to himself, in the storehouse of his memory, which was beginning to seem infinite.

SINCE BECOMING A PRISONER, BRASSE HAD STOPPED LOOKING AT
himself in the mirror. The only exception he'd made had been
when getting ready to meet Baśka, before she disappeared from
the camp. Not anymore. Even when his glance fell on his own
reflection in a window, he managed not to look at himself or to
assess the changes on his face wrought by time and fear.

Much as he might avoid confronting the realities of his
external appearance, the more time passed, the more he looked
inside himself, something that happened every time he studied
the photographs he had developed. He felt that each picture was
calling to him, which made him suffer greatly and come to understand the state of his mind, the state of his soul.

One evening, Brasse was in the laboratory alone, assessing the quality of the detail in a photo of an enormous pile of naked corpses being consumed by flames. Were there a hundred of them? No, they were so thin that there must have been a far greater number.

As he ran his eyes over the atrocious scene, he felt agitation in the parts of his heart that were still alive and sensitive. In his mind, there was no such sensation: it tried, as always, to keep such feelings at bay. It didn't always succeed, though, and sometimes worked without his permission, storing up thoughts and images in a secret chamber only for them to come tumbling out as soon as he lowered his guard. This would often happen at dawn, if he made the mistake of waking up even so much as a minute before the wake-up call.

Looking now at this picture of the immense pyre, Brasse knew it wouldn't be long before he was assailed by the knowledge that a similar end awaited him. And as usual, he wouldn't stop there: he'd imagine himself naked, dead, and cold, then finally burned by the flames that would eliminate him definitively.

These pictures, taken by Walter and Hofmann, showed heaps of bodies being burned outside for the sake of speed, because the crematorium ovens couldn't keep up. The images would end up in the two men's personal collections. Brasse had already seen similar photographs, because a few days earlier, he had secretly developed and printed others of the same scene, taken by innocent hands, not with the same bloodthirsty passion as demonstrated by his superiors.

A few prisoners from Block 17 had taken them, with the help of Mieczysław Morawa, Brasse's friend in the crematorium who had informed him of his uncle's death. These prisoners wanted to create a permanent record of the horrors they were witnessing, and Morawa had asked his friends at the Identification Service for a portable camera so they could photograph the burning of the bodies from the window of their block.

It had been a dangerous but necessary operation. Brasse and his team had been happy to help and had been able to do so without taking too many risks. Now, the prisoners told them, the pictures would be sent out of the camp and be seen by the rest of the world.

So there was still a resistance in Auschwitz. There were people who thought of something beyond their own survival.

Brasse put Walter's photographs in an envelope marked "confidential," sank back in his chair, and stretched out his legs, staring vacantly in front of him.

He sighed. Yes, he was tired, and he felt old. Above all, he felt contaminated by his long years spent in the service of the SS. But he was alive and had a chance of surviving longer. So would joining the resistance—as he had now decided to do—really be worth it?

Of course his mother would like to see him again, and his brothers, his people. Was it right to think of them still? He had already played his part: he'd defended his honor as a Polish citizen, he'd saved a few lives by taking prisoners on at the Identification Service, he'd managed to prevent a few acts of excessive violence, and he'd shared his food and treated desperate prisoners humanely. Could he do more? Should he? It was one thing to reduce suffering where he could; it was another to resist and struggle for victory. Was there any point? He would be putting his team, for whom he felt responsible, in danger.

He often thought of two heroes, two Polish men to be proud of. He'd met them in the camp, and they'd been shot, up against the wall of death, in October of the preceding year. They were officers from the defeated army—political prisoners of some importance—and the Germans had tempted them with offers of collaboration. The men had remained faithful to their beliefs, and instead of trying to save their skins, they had headed the resistance. They passed news to the outside world, helped prisoners who needed to lie about their real identities, and did their best to support the weakest by persuading their companions to share food with them.

Brasse remembered them well: just men, full of integrity. He'd learned their names when they were sent to Block 26 to be photographed and registered: Colonel Teofil Dziama and Captain Tadeusz Lisowski. Lisowski had given a false name, though, and the men in Block 26 had only discovered this long after. His real name was Paolone.

Brasse had admired them and rejoiced in their small successes. Then he had cried, without being able to reveal his sadness to anyone, when he'd learned of their arrests and immediate executions.

He had been even more disturbed to learn how they had been

singled out: there was an SS informer in the midst of the prisoners in the camp. He was another Pole by the name of Stefan Ołpiński. Everyone knew about him. He had a little room of his own in Block 25, where he slept with a few other men, and he was often given excellent meals from the kitchens reserved for SS officers. He had denounced the two brave Polish officers and innumerable other men over the years.

Brasse opened the envelope again and looked at the pictures of the fire where so many innocent lives had ended. Death. Was that the inevitable fate of all prisoners in the camp? Was it also his fate, whatever he did, for good or ill?

Even Ołpiński was dead now. A few months earlier, at the end of 1943, he had caught typhus during the epidemic and had met the same end as Ruski, left to die by the doctors. This time, it was Polish doctors in Block 20 who'd done everything they could not to cure him: they'd pretended to treat him because, unlike Ruski, Ołpiński was useful to the Germans. So the traitor had been killed by their "solicitous" care...

This too was resistance, Brasse reflected.

But the final reckoning wasn't encouraging. In this factory of death, heroes and traitors met the same end, and no amount of resistance could slow down the machine's workings. This was just as true in the world outside. No partisan force seemed capable of disrupting—even for just a few days—the railway lines that transported people to Auschwitz, so the Germans continued to carry out their project undisturbed.

Over the last few weeks, for example, there had been a new development: far more Italian prisoners were arriving at the camp. It was a great surprise—even though the Germans had been abandoned by their allies, they seemed stronger than ever, and when Walter and his fellow officers talked among themselves, they often expressed pride in being able to win the war by themselves.

All things considered, the pictures he had printed destroyed all hope. That pile of corpses consumed by fire was undeniable testimony to the fact that the pace of killing was increasing. More and more prisoners were being murdered, and thousands continued to arrive. The Germans might not be winning the war as quickly as they had thought, but there was no letup in the extermination, which was so important a goal that ever more resources were being directed toward it.

Brasse heard the door of the block open and closed the envelope quickly. He had no desire to discuss the images. He would deliver them, and that would be all. He wouldn't even reply if Walter asked his opinion about them.

But it wasn't Walter at the door.

"Brasse, come out!"

It was Josefsberg, the circumcised boy who risked death every time he took a shower, and he seemed agitated. It was after the curfew, and everyone should have been in their barracks, asleep. Usually nobody disturbed Brasse at this time, when he lingered in the laboratory to complete his work.

"Come in. I've finished."

Josefsberg stared at him with bright eyes. He looked feverish.

"Has something happened?" Brasse asked.

"Didn't you hear?"

"No."

"There've been explosions. We definitely heard them. Tadek's sure it's American or British planes dropping bombs."

"Where?"

"On the Buna-Werke factory. It makes sense, doesn't it? They make rubber for military use there…"

Brasse and Josefsberg went outside, headed for the shadows between two blocks, and listened intently. It was dark now, and the sky was silent. At first, they didn't hear anything. Then came a thud and a distant rumble. The ground even seemed to tremble slightly.

"Hear that? Hear that?"

Josefsberg was excited, but Brasse was wary.

"Be quiet! Do you want someone to hear us?"

They listened again. Now came what they thought sounded like the roar of airplanes, but it could have been a trick of the mind.

"Lots of prisoners work at the Buna," Brasse said. "Including British prisoners of war. And they work in the evening too. Do you really think the Americans or British would bomb their own people?"

"I don't know. Perhaps they warned them and told them to pretend they're ill…"

At that moment, some much louder and closer explosions

took them by surprise. They even saw flashes of light—outside the camp but not very far away.

This time, it was Brasse's turn to show excitement.

"It's the German antiaircraft guns! They're shooting at enemy planes!"

"Antiaircraft guns?" Josefsberg asked.

"Yes, I heard the Germans were building antiaircraft artillery stations around the camp. I didn't believe it, but listen—they're shooting!"

"They might bomb us too," Josefsberg said worriedly.

If only they would, thought Brasse. But he had to admit that the prospect of dying at the hands of the Allies after surviving for so many years seemed a cruel twist of fate.

They heard a squadron approaching and ran to shelter in the darkness of Block 25. The other men were already there in their bunks but not sleeping. They were discussing the situation in whispers, full of hope.

"It isn't the first time they've come," Myszkowski insisted. "They prefer to bomb during the day, if possible, so they can be more precise."

Others couldn't believe what they'd heard. They accused Myszkowski of giving too much sway to rumors spread around by the camp resistance to give prisoners faith in their activities. At the mention of the resistance, Brasse remembered the news he'd been thinking of before Josefsberg had interrupted him. For months and months—four years—he had suppressed all hope for fear of deluding himself, for fear of going mad, but now he felt it rise within him.

Myszkowski, meanwhile, was trying to dispel his companions' doubts.

"But don't you understand? The Germans built the antiaircraft guns precisely because they're getting worried. The war's been going on for nearly five years, and finally the Allies are strong enough to bomb occupied territory. It's clearly a sign that things are going badly for the Nazis. Even the Russians are on the counterattack, and they're getting closer to our boundaries. I know that for certain."

Silence. Minds working furiously in the darkness. A secret battle against hope.

"We need to know more," was all Brasse said. It came out sounding like a definitive decision, an order, as though he were organizing a vitally important operation.

In the morning, however, they didn't need to seek out news. Walter came into the laboratory with the obvious intention of communicating the developments to them formally. He was beaming.

"Well, late yesterday evening, the Americans thought they'd give us a fright by dropping more bombs on the Buna-Werke. Didn't you hear anything?"

Brasse saved the others from answering this difficult question by choosing the most prudent response. "By that time, we're all tired and sound asleep, Herr Hauptscharführer. I did hear something, but I thought it must have been a storm."

Walter looked at Brasse suspiciously, as he always did when he suspected the photographer was making fun of him. But the news he had to impart was far more important and pleasant than this misgiving.

"Anyway," Walter continued, "the upshot is that the antiaircraft guns around the camp kept them from coming anywhere near Auschwitz and Birkenau. But the best part is that those idiots did manage to hit the factory, and in doing so, they killed over thirty British prisoners of war."

The members of the kommando exchanged quick glances, trying not to draw attention to themselves. Was this true?

Walter saw what they were thinking.

"You will soon have ample proof that what I'm telling you is true. Don't worry. We know that rumors are going around the camp and that there are some who are managing to get news from outside. They will soon be eliminated, as others have been before them. But this time, it's best that you know the truth and, above all, that you fully understand the consequences of the error our enemies have made."

Brodka and Myszkowski were still puzzled, but Brasse understood what Walter meant.

Walter puffed out his chest and began to explain more clearly.

"Our military commanders will soon send a list to the enemy commanders, with details of all the men killed by their own aircraft. Our men will also make sure the news gets to the United States and Great Britain, even though it would normally be a military secret. Those butchers will think again before taking their lives in their hands in the face of our antiaircraft guns and barrage balloons just to come and kill their own countrymen!"

Brasse nodded silently, but Walter wasn't satisfied.

"What do you say, Brasse? Am I not right?"

"I think…you are right, sir."

"I am, believe me. And let it be known in the camp that none of you will be saved by enemy bombardment. The sooner you shed your illusions, the better."

Walter saluted and left, even happier than he'd been when he arrived. He'd enjoyed seeing the disappointed faces of the Erkennungsdienst, and he'd enjoyed the spectacle of the power he wielded over them. As for the kommando, after Walter left, they didn't dare look one another in the eye for fear of seeing their own bitter disappointment reflected in every face.

2 6

A ONE-DOLLAR NOTE. BRASSE PLACED IT CAREFULLY ON the table, taking care to hold it flat and still before putting a clean glass plate over it. Then he maneuvered his lens so that it was exactly parallel with the surface to be photographed. The small, precious rectangle was perfectly illuminated by two lamps, and George Washington gazed at Brasse with the noble expression of a good man who has fulfilled his life's great mission.

Walter had given precise instructions. He wanted a clear, exact copy of both sides of the note. The brand-new opaque projector would then be used to look at images of it on a screen that had been set up in the studio just the previous day. These projected images, greatly enlarged, would be used by a new colleague at the Identification Service. The kommando still went by that name and continued to produce pictures of prisoners and soldiers, but now it was working on something very different, and it had nothing to do with photographing people: it was an object that needed to be reproduced.

Brasse worked with absolute concentration, trying not to let himself be distracted by the thousand thoughts whirling in his mind.

The whole operation was shrouded in absolute secrecy. Only Brasse and Myszkowski were involved: them and their new colleague. He was a Jew, and this was enough to indicate the exceptional importance of the operation.

"This is Herr Leo Haas," Walter had said. "He's an expert artist and graphic designer, and he's joining our kommando. You will show him our equipment and give him your utmost cooperation on this job. You must never talk about it to other prisoners or even to other camp officials with the exception of myself. Nobody must disturb his work, and you should consider yourselves at his service. If you have any doubts whatsoever, you ask me. Understood?"

The man who had followed Walter into the room and who was now standing among them was about forty years old and had the air of a gentle schoolmaster. The number on his arm, as Brasse and Myszkowski knew well, indicated that he had only recently arrived at the camp, but his face and body bore the signs of lengthy privation.

"I've come from the Theresienstadt ghetto," he said without any further explanation, as though that name, which the two

Poles were hearing for the first time, was enough to evoke untold suffering.

Brasse realized that Haas expected the transfer to Auschwitz to bring about a great improvement in his life. The fact that he, a Jew, had been entrusted with an important secret mission seemed to confirm this expectation. Brasse decided not to upset his new colleague with any more questions.

"Where shall we start?"

It was immediately apparent that the man was extremely competent and had received detailed instructions about what was required of him.

"I'll draw exact copies of American banknotes. You'll photograph them and create negatives, from which we'll create photographic plates for printing more notes. Fake ones, obviously."

Myszkowski didn't understand. "And what will they do with them?"

The man smiled at the boy's naivete. "They'll try to flood the United States with a huge influx of fake currency to create confusion—or worse."

"So it's an act of war," Brasse concluded.

"Yes, an act of war."

They hadn't commented further. This work was the new price to be paid for their survival, and that was that. Nevertheless, as Brasse took the pictures of the notes, a persistent thought tormented him: in the end, they'd succeeded in making him fight on their side. With his own weapons, of course. But still…

"All right?"

Haas fit well into his role as head of the operation. Thanks to some food and rest, his face took on a healthier color, and his back straightened as the days went by. His hair was now clean and combed back. He was evidently enjoying this unexpected well-being and the hope that he might become indispensable to his jailers.

"All right," Brasse replied. "You'll be able to start drawing this evening."

As soon as the enlargement was ready, Haas set to work.

He was happy with Brasse's reproductions: every detail was clear, and the proportions were just right. Brasse had managed to stop the lens from tilting even slightly, which would have resulted in major distortions on the enlarged image.

Brasse watched with interest as Haas worked. He divided the image on the banknote into six equal sections, then drew each section on a large sheet of paper, which took a long time. Then, Brasse photographed all six drawings and reduced them to the exact size of the original note. A slide of each section was projected onto the pearly white screen using the opaque projector, and every detail of Haas's drawing was compared with the authentic dollar bill. If, after careful examination, the details corresponded, Haas approved that section. If, however, he noticed the slightest discrepancy, he made a new drawing of that section, working on it until he was completely satisfied. Then Brasse could photograph it again.

This work went on for five days: Haas drew, and Brasse

photographed and projected the drawing; Haas compared, identified errors, went back to his drawings, and Brasse photographed them again. During this time, there were hardly any visitors to Block 26, and those who did come were limited to Walter and other officers from the Political Department. The other prisoners who worked with Brasse in the Identification Service were excused from their duties.

Finally, it seemed to everyone that the drawings were perfect. Brasse agreed and had to endure friendly pats on the shoulder from his superiors, who clearly considered him their colleague in this operation.

Walter ordered Myszkowski to have the negatives ready so the photographic plates could be prepared. They couldn't make these themselves, so they sent the negatives to a laboratory in the town of Auschwitz that had agreed to work for the camp authorities.

A detachment of two Polish prisoners, expert printers from Warsaw, was sent to oversee the creation of the plates and then the printing in a second laboratory. They used Brasse's negatives to create the three copies they needed (three in all because dollars contained three colors: black, green, and red).

Walter boasted to Brasse and Haas that the SS had managed to get their hands on the perfect paper to make notes, and nobody would be able to distinguish them from real ones. Indeed, their very first attempts produced perfect fakes. Brasse was given ten of these counterfeit banknotes, and he photographed them, then projected them onto the screen once more while Haas carried out scrupulous checks, watched by a group of German officers.

It was done. The SS celebrated the success of the operation and were lavish in their praise of the Jewish artist and Brasse for producing "our" dollars. Walter even shook Haas's hand and gave him what Walter clearly considered to be a compliment: "Say what you like about you Jews, you can't say you don't know a thing or two about money!"

Haas didn't reply.

As far as Brasse could gather, printing the counterfeit currency continued at top speed over the next few days, but they weren't told any more about it.

Two weeks later, Haas received orders to get ready to leave. He was to go to another camp: Sachsenhausen.

"I'll be drawing sterling," he said to Brasse in his usual neutral tone, like an employee moving from one job to the next. "Let's hope they have a photographer as good as you there."

Brasse said nothing. It didn't even cross his mind to try to prevent any of this from happening. Haas didn't have any choice in the matter. He had to do his best to survive, and his art made that possible. It was the same thing Brasse had been doing for years.

"Will this war end one day?" he asked the artist. "Will we manage to escape from it?"

Haas squeezed his shoulder. "As you can see, the Germans are giving it all they've got." Then he gave Brasse a conspiratorial look.

"All I know is that to make perfect sterling takes us much, much longer. They're much more complex notes. You see what I mean?"

Brasse smiled and nodded. Yes, more complex notes, which meant days and days—or weeks and weeks—of work. All time won from death.

At the same time, Brasse was still pondering the idea that had consoled him during all those days spent in the laboratory: how to let the resistance know about what the Germans, with Brasse's own help, were doing to win the war.

When Haas left, life in the Erkennungsdienst returned to normal: pictures of Slovak or Slovenian deportees and new political prisoners arriving from all over Europe, resistance fighters whom the Germans were keen to register very carefully. Brasse occasionally managed to exchange a few words with them, and he discovered that often they were simply ordinary people arrested as an act of revenge or because they were related to someone who was part of the clandestine fight against the Nazis.

One day, Walter came into the laboratory with two kapos, Germans imprisoned for committing common crimes.

"These men are about to be released," he explained, his expression grave. "We need to prepare documents for them so they can carry out a special mission." He lowered his voice to emphasize the seriousness of what he was about to add. "And, Brasse, I'm counting on your discretion with regard to these men and other volunteers I'll be sending you over the next few weeks. You are to give the negatives of their portraits straight to me, and under no circumstances are you to tell anyone they've left the camp. This requires the same level of secrecy as the operation with the dollars. Do you understand?"

Brasse didn't ask questions, and Walter said nothing more to him about the special mission these men leaving the camp were to undertake. However, some of the chosen prisoners couldn't keep their mouths shut. They came in pairs and thought nobody could understand when they spoke to one another in German. Some even boasted openly about their mission in front of the prisoners in Block 26.

"We're going to kill rebels," they would say. "Poles, Jewish scum. Like the ones in Warsaw last year who rebelled and killed a couple of SS men and Ukrainians who were working for us. But they all ended up dead themselves—slaughtered like rats. The Germans went from house to house with flamethrowers and drove them all out. They threw canisters of asphyxiant gas into the buildings, chucked gasoline all over the ground floors, and lit a match. Anyone still alive after that came running out with their arses on fire. The Germans deported them all, and now they've finished the job and gassed them all. Thousands of them came here, not looking as cocky as they used to..."

This was the talk of people who were certain of victory, who didn't doubt themselves for a moment. They exchanged these stories excitedly, looking forward to getting involved in the brawling themselves. One claimed to have been chosen because he spoke Polish and would be able to gather information from ordinary people. He said that Poles were idiots and easy to hoodwink. Another even mentioned the name of the person in charge of them.

"We're going to join General Zelewski's special unit."

"Is he Polish, with a name like that?"

"No, German. Apparently his full name's something like von dem Bach-Zelewski."

"Oh, an aristocrat, then."

"I don't care if he's an aristocrat or not, I just want to get out of here. If they give me food and a decent gun, I'll kill as many partisans as they like."

"Exactly. And we know a thing or two about gas, don't we?"

They laughed, rubbing their hands at the thought of the deal they were making.

Some of them came to the studio already dressed in civilian clothes, wearing sports jackets and hunting caps. A sort of improvised uniform, perhaps, or maybe just a code for the photographs, a way of identifying the members of the emerging secret squad. Brasse remained impassive, doing his job as usual and pretending not to understand a word. When he needed to ask one of the men to stand still or change pose, he barely said more than "*bitte*" and pronounced that badly.

Day after day, he sent the prints and negatives to Walter and Hofmann, but he memorized the names of the men being released, which were printed on their documents. Had it been possible, he would have made copies of the photographs and hidden them away, but he had only the men's names and descriptions. Still, he had decided he would pass on even this small amount of information.

There were very few prisoners Brasse knew he could trust, and he tried to contact one of them—Dunikowski. The man was an artist, painter, and sculptor who worked for the Germans and made the most of their faith in him by coordinating clandestine organizations among the prisoners.

But Brasse was to be disappointed.

"Dunikowski? No chance. They've just arrested him. He's in the cells in Block 11. They want to starve him to death. They're furious because they feel betrayed. They gave him every possible privilege, they're saying, and all the time, he was fooling them. We're going to impossible lengths to get food and water to him without being discovered. If he manages to hold on until the liberation, it'll be a miracle."

The man giving Brasse this information was a prisoner who didn't want to give his real name and kept the number tattooed on his arm well hidden.

Brasse gave a start. "Liberation? What liberation?"

The man looked annoyed. "What are you talking about?"

"You said…"

"I didn't say anything at all. Go back to your work and leave off looking for Dunikowski. Tell yourself he's dead, all right?"

"But I wanted to help you."

"There's nothing you can to do help us. As far as you're concerned, we don't exist. If I need help, I'll come and find you. You've got plenty of food in Block 26, haven't you?"

Brasse nodded. "Yes, but I've also got important information about secret SS operations against the resistance and the Allies."

The man looked at him through narrowed eyes. Brasse felt he was being sized up.

"We'll see" was the man's only answer. "Wait for a call. I need to ask a few people about you."

And he went off without saying goodbye.

Brasse returned to his block, wondering if he'd been unwise to put himself forward. Above all, though, he was puzzled. He was trying to reveal the counterfeit dollar operation and the secret enlistment of antiresistance hirelings, and this man was asking him for a bit of food!

But perhaps those who ran the prisoners' clandestine activities couldn't trust him straightaway. After all, he worked closely with the SS. He took photographs of them, enlarged and printed their pictures and portraits, and had been receiving favors from them for years now. These were unimaginable privileges for most prisoners.

He went back into the studio.

"There are some Slovaks waiting to be photographed."

Brodka carried on the usual work without any hesitation.

Brasse, too, went straight back to the routine, as he had done every day for over four years. He didn't say anything to anybody about the conversation he'd just had. It had been too dangerous. And probably useless. Better just to carry on surviving.

ONE DAY, MALTZ—WHO NEVER BEAT HIS KOMMANDO because he wasn't allowed to but who hated them just the same and told them so as often as he could—disappeared.

The Identification Service waited a few days before trying to find out what had happened—it was always wiser not to show any interest when something changed. Brasse wondered if Maltz had also enlisted in the special squad, but Brodka had a different theory.

"He must've told people about that dream he had."

Myszkowski was incredulous. "Do you think so? Surely not! Maltz is mad and dangerous, but he's survived five years in this camp. He must know how to keep his mouth shut."

"But you saw how strange he was about it. He was all excited.

It was as if he had a special mission: the prophet of Germany's destiny! Sent by the gods to open the Nazis' eyes before it's too late!"

"Silence!"

As usual, Brasse didn't want to take any risks. He'd tried especially hard not to draw attention to Block 26, and his nerves were raw.

"Come on, Wilhelm. We're only joking."

"I don't care. If it's true that Maltz had that dream and went around telling everyone about it, then he really is mad. But let's not talk about it, please."

It was true that the last time their kapo had come to see them, he had seemed to be having some kind of nervous crisis, and he'd made them all feel uncomfortable.

"Brasse, you won't believe this!" he'd said. "You neither, Tadek. Listen…"

When Maltz was happy, it meant he had bad news to tell them. The kommando men were always busy and not interested in going around the camp, keeping an eye on what was going on, but the kapo liked watching new arrivals, the ever-hastier selection processes, and the executions. He also enjoyed seeing the effect his discoveries had on the little scaredy-cats in Block 26. He especially disliked Brasse and was always hoping to provoke him, to make him react and say something compromising that Maltz could then use against him to their superiors. And lately, Maltz had been keeping an especially close eye on Brasse, who was aware of all this suspicion and vigilance and feared it. Perhaps his efforts to collaborate with the prisoners undermining the Germans, which were just now coming to fruition, would be discovered.

"You'll never guess what I dreamed last night," Maltz began. "I can still see it all, as though I were still dreaming."

The prisoners had readied themselves to listen, prudently feigning interest, but it soon became impossible to remain indifferent.

"I saw that the war was over and Germany was beaten. There was barbed wire all around. And who do you think was behind that wire, as though they were in a concentration camp?"

The kommando members watched him uneasily. Josefsberg, who had initially been more curious than the others, pretended to remember an urgent job that needed doing.

"Wait, listen to me!" Maltz barked.

There was nothing for it; they'd have to hear him out. The kapo at least had the sense to lower his voice.

"Behind the barbed wire were Hitler, Himmler, and the whole lot of them! I saw them clearly with my own eyes! What do you say to that?"

Nobody wanted to say anything. Brasse looked at the triangle sewn onto the kapo's uniform. He was a political prisoner, and they all knew he'd been imprisoned, even before the war, for being a Communist. It would seem that his old vocation as an enemy of the regime was reasserting itself. Or was he just trying to prove that he was ready for big changes to come? Was he making it all up to provoke them? For a Communist, it was extremely risky to be talking this way. But Maltz really seemed to have forgotten any sense of caution.

"Well? Isn't it extraordinary?"

Brasse had to admit it: Maltz wasn't acting according to any rational plan. He wasn't trying to arouse their enthusiasm in order to denounce them. And he wasn't trying to persuade them that he'd decided to collaborate with the camp resistance, perhaps suspecting that Brasse had useful contacts there. No, he was really struck by this dream, full of enthusiasm about it, as though he'd had a revelation.

Brasse looked around. As usual, the others were waiting for him to get them out of this embarrassing situation.

"Kapo Maltz, with all due respect, it was just a dream."

"Rubbish, Brasse! I've been here for years, and I've never had a dream like that before! I saw them—do you understand? They were hanging their heads in despair! They were afraid!"

They needed to calm him down. Walter or Hofmann could appear at any moment.

"All right, Kapo Maltz, we understand."

"Ha! You don't understand at all! You don't know anything! You're stuck in here like caged mice. And this is where they'll find you and kill you, as soon as they start cleaning everything up. It's over. Don't you see? It's over!"

Brasse got to his feet.

"May I go back to work?"

The others were already dispersing, not waiting for permission.

Maltz went right up to Brasse so their faces were only a few inches apart. His breath stank of alcohol; he'd had a lot to drink, but there was another kind of poison in his eyes, an insane mixture of rage and joy.

"Carry on like that, Brasse," he whispered, furious now. Brasse feared he would hit him, but Maltz was lost in his own unhinged thoughts. "Carry on like that, and we'll see which of us survives."

When he had gone, nobody said anything for at least half an hour. They acted as though nothing had happened and didn't speak about the incident.

Now Maltz had disappeared.

They waited a few days, certain he would reappear, but they never saw him again. Eventually, they spotted his name on a list of prisoners who'd been shot and had already vanished into the crematorium.

As soon as he had the chance, Brasse asked Hofmann for news of their kapo, pretending not to know about the execution.

"Herr Hofmann, what's become of Franz Maltz?"

The corporal smiled. "Kapo Maltz won't be coming back."

Brasse maintained a polite silence, waiting for more details. Hofmann pretended to ignore him, but he obviously wanted to say more.

"What is it, Brasse? Is there something else you want to know?"

"No, sir. We…"

"Let's say that he's gone to dream elsewhere. Is that enough for you?"

That was enough.

But the kommando couldn't help fretting over what had happened. They had endless discussions about who could have let it get out about the dream.

Brodka swore that he and all the men in Block 26 had been discreet.

"Trust us, Brasse! None of us said anything. We didn't have anything to gain by it."

That was true. So who had talked?

Wawrzyniak tried to find out more from a friend of his who knew an obliging kapo. He relayed to the others what he discovered, and when they heard his story, they were even more incredulous than they had been when Maltz had told them about his dream.

"It's already legendary in the camp. The kapos are all talking about it, but the prisoners don't understand what it's all about. We seem to be the only ones who know the truth."

"And what is the truth?"

"Maltz went and talked about his dream to one of the police commissioners in the camp—someone who can't stand Communists. Who knows? Maybe Maltz sobered up and regretted telling us about it. Maybe he decided to go and denounce himself and make a joke out of the whole thing before word got out."

"If that was the case, he could just have told us to keep quiet. We've always got along all right with him. We didn't have any reason to get rid of him only to have him replaced by someone much worse."

Brodka was right. They couldn't understand it.

"Could it be that he really didn't trust us at all?"

Brasse could confirm the truth of this. "No, he didn't. Whatever his reason for telling that commissioner about his dream, it never occurred to him to come to some agreement with us. He hated us. He always hated us. So he was afraid of us. That's the long and the short of it."

And that was the end of Maltz. The Identification Service all got up and went back to work, knowing they would never discuss this episode again.

Brasse gave a sigh of relief. Maltz had been breathing down his neck, and sooner or later, that would have become a dangerous thing.

That evening, though, Brasse couldn't get to sleep. He kept seeing Maltz's eyes staring into his own, in all their unhinged madness. This madness was hope, long-suppressed hope that had finally developed into insanity. In the climate of increasing expectation that was spreading around the camp despite all efforts to suppress it, it was no wonder someone like Maltz had been driven mad.

Brasse had this madness to thank for freeing him from an enemy. His good fortune continued, and he had decided to test it without hesitating any longer. Was this courage? Or was it madness of a different variety?

He wanted to live, as he always had, but he didn't *just* want to live. He wanted to achieve something good. And that meant he was now ready to risk death. Now that everything might be about to come to an end.

It was why he passed the secret information about the counterfeit dollars and the names of the men leaving to fight rebels to the resistance. Now that he'd done it, his doubts subsided. He felt good, that was all. He was finally performing his own act of rebellion against the horror and the absurdity.

As he thought of all this, a memory suddenly surfaced from some forgotten part of his mind.

It was spring, 1941 perhaps? Yes, over three years ago now. A century. Or perhaps just the brief flutter of a few calendar pages, each of which were interchangeable with any of the others in the repetitive litany of death that spread over every season, a litany that was silenced and distanced from the mind by the obstinate monotony of labor.

The spring months in Auschwitz had all been the same, but now, lying there in the dark accompanied by Wawrzyniak's incessant snoring, Brasse remembered one particular day when he had looked out the window of Block 26 and seen a group of twelve monks in Franciscan habits filing past. They hadn't yet been forced to wear the camp uniform, and for a moment, he had the strange feeling of witnessing an age-old spectacle: a procession in a monastery, a place of peace.

The monks were brought into the Erkennungsdienst. The

order was to take the usual photographs in three poses, and the twelve men obeyed Brasse's requests with calm composure. He and his colleagues—even those who had never been particularly religious—had instinctively treated the men with respect. As he took the pictures, he wondered how these men of God would live in the hell of the camp and whether they would maintain their serene purposefulness once deprived of their habits.

Stanisław Trałka was preparing the handwritten cards to go with the pictures, as usual, but for some reason, the SS hadn't prepared a complete list of names. They had ordered the prisoners to declare any names that could be attributed to them once they were at the Identification Service. Perhaps the Germans feared that some of them might try to use the names they had taken on as monks and thus hide their true origins.

One of them seemed to be their leader: the others looked to him before answering any questions and obviously put their faith in him—especially the younger ones. When the leader's turn came, Brasse heard him speak to Trałka in a firm voice.

"I am Father Kolbe," he said. "Maximilian Rajmund Kolbe is my name."

Brasse realized that he had heard that name before. It was a childhood memory. Kolbe wrote for a Franciscan magazine for children called *The Little Knight of the Immaculate Conception*. Like many of his friends, Brasse had read it as a boy, as part of his upbringing as a good Christian.

Father Kolbe sat in the revolving chair. Brasse gave him a

smile, and the monk returned it, his eyes tired and sad but illuminated with a spark of goodness and brightening with interest at this unexpected smile.

When all the photographs were finished, Kolbe thanked the team, and Brasse was sorry not to have been able to talk to him a little.

By the next day, the Germans had taken the monks' clothes, dressed the men in camp uniforms, and assigned them to collecting and transporting corpses. Brasse didn't see them again after that.

Then, one morning in August, he had witnessed the monk's action.

Two days earlier, a prisoner had escaped. Fritzsch, the deputy camp commandant at that stage, had immediately ordered reprisal killings: if the fugitive didn't reappear or if he wasn't recaptured within twenty-four hours, ten of his companions from Block 14 would be starved to death. The prisoner didn't reappear, so during roll call, Fritzsch carried out his threat and began to select the victims. Brasse was there, as they all were, standing to attention, and he had seen and heard everything.

Fritzsch was walking slowly along the row of wretched men, lined up waiting for death. Every so often, he stopped.

"You. Take a step forward," he would say without batting an eye. And the man would somehow manage to take a step and stay there in front of everyone, still standing at attention.

Then the commandant would move on again and call on another prisoner.

It was terrible. None of those picked out said a word, none seemed to tremble, none threw themselves to the ground in panic. Perhaps they still hoped, up to the very end, that Fritzsch would change his mind.

Then something happened. Fritzsch selected another man, who began to shout.

"Mother of God, no! I've got a wife and children! No!"

It was harrowing. Brasse thought Fritzsch would use violence to silence the man who was disrupting his selection process, but something quite different occurred. A prisoner from Block 14 began to make his way between the rows of men without being called. He walked right up to the commandant without asking his permission and spoke to him in German, loudly and steadily enough for everyone to hear.

"Let me take this prisoner's place," he said. "I am old, and I have no family."

Brasse, like everyone else, couldn't take his eyes off the man who stood in front of the commandant, his head held high. It was Father Kolbe.

They all knew the SS didn't tolerate gestures of solidarity, but the inconceivable happened. The man who had been selected had fallen to his knees and was still sobbing desperately. Fritzsch looked at Kolbe with all the hatred he could muster and asked his name and origin.

Nobody heard the reply, but it must have pleased the commandant, because he immediately ordered the ten condemned men to be taken away, including Kolbe, while the sobbing prisoner was allowed to live. As they removed Kolbe, the SS soldiers looked at the monk, unrecognizable in his dirty uniform, with smiles of derision.

What happened next was only heard in camp rumors. Kolbe died in the bunker of Block 13 after ten days of complete starvation. They'd given him a lethal injection to finish him off.

Some had called this gesture heroic and senseless.

Brasse, who now, three years later, couldn't sleep in his comfortable bunk in Block 25, remembered with shame that he'd agreed, then, that sacrificing oneself in Auschwitz would simply mean that any prisoner who had been spared would survive only a few weeks longer—they would die just the same.

And yet.

Years had passed. Who could say if the prisoner Kolbe saved was still alive? Kolbe himself was now only ash borne away by the wind. In the meantime, the Germans must surely have closed down his little magazine for children. Perhaps they'd also burned down his monastery or requisitioned it for another purpose. Brasse turned over and tried to sleep. Things in Auschwitz happened, and that was all there was to it. And then other things happened. The end.

Nothing was left of Kolbe, but Brasse was thinking about him. The memory of that great sacrifice, made without hesitation, remained vivid in his memory. It was a memory that tormented him now, at night, but also consoled him and encouraged him to go on. He thought of the information he'd passed to the resistance. It was the right thing to have done. So now he could sleep.

28

BRASSE POINTED OUT THE DEFECTS IN A FEW PRINTS OF photographs that Walter and Hofmann had taken on the ramp where the trains arrived at the camp. As he had predicted, the officers weren't happy with the images, and he easily convinced them that they would obtain better outdoor photographs if they were to set their portable cameras on a tripod. With something to lean on, Brasse argued, the pictures of moving prisoners would be less blurred, and fewer would have to be discarded because they looked as though they'd been taken carelessly, in a hurry.

Walter listened carefully, as he always did when Brasse was giving him professional advice. Walter was very attached to his collection of pictures of deportees getting off trains and of the first selection process—of families split up, the children crying and clinging to the skirts of desperate mothers who watched their husbands being taken away, not yet knowing they would be the first to be taken, then and there, straight to the gas chambers.

Brasse's two superiors were grateful for his advice, and he suggested that he himself should arrange to have a tripod ready for them at Birkenau, where they had said they wanted to photograph groups of female prisoners going to work: proof of the camp's undiminished efficiency. They liked this idea, and he assured them that it could all be arranged at no inconvenience to themselves.

"You'll find everything ready tomorrow morning," he said. "With your permission, I'll have the tripod taken to where you want it. Then we'll come and get it when you've finished or have it brought back by someone in charge of transport in the camp."

Walter didn't suspect anything: he was used to this kind of collaboration from his most professional and thorough worker.

That evening, Brasse stayed late in the lab, with the excuse of finalizing the printing of a few enlargements. He opened the door to a prisoner he didn't know.

"Good evening. I'm Jurek."

That was all he said, and he kept the number on his arm well covered. Brasse knew that wasn't his real name. He also knew he'd just have to trust him and not allow himself to be paralyzed by the thought that if this man was an informer, Brasse's fate was already sealed.

The prisoner had brought a military satchel with him. It was full and looked heavy.

"Here it is," he said, resting his load on the work desk. "Are you the one in charge of getting this to Birkenau?"

"One of you will take it there," Brasse replied, "but in a case belonging to this block." He pulled out the tripod case, opened it, and showed it, empty, to his visitor.

Jurek looked inside and nodded solemnly. "That should do. And the Germans won't want to look inside?"

"No. We'll seal it up and put a label on it saying it's a piece of equipment from the Erkennungsdienst for Hauptscharführer Walter. No one will dare open it, except the women who've already been told it's on its way. We've already thought of how to get the tripod to Birkenau. Then, when the goods have been delivered, the case will be there, ready to bring the tripod back here. Will that work?"

Jurek was satisfied. "Yes, that'll work. The SS and the kapos won't dare interfere with the Political Department. And everyone knows that Walter goes around the camp taking photographs."

The pair set to work transferring little bags full of white pills and powder from the satchel to the case. Brasse didn't ask questions. He'd assumed it would be food they'd be transporting to Birkenau, where hunger was now becoming unbearable, but it was something else.

The stranger saw his surprise. "Contraband medicine," he explained. "We're trying to help the women who are ill. The Germans don't care for them anymore, not even to get them well enough to go back to work."

Brasse was both pleased and amazed. So it wasn't just stuff that they'd somehow managed to steal from the camp kitchens.

It was goods from outside, valuable goods. Getting them into the camp must have required money and accomplices, free citizens who were prepared to risk their lives to save prisoners.

He would have liked to know more, but the transfer only took a few minutes, and Jurek got ready to leave immediately.

The two men shook hands.

"Thank you," Jurek said. "This has been a great help to us."

Brasse didn't reply. He didn't feel like a hero. He could do it, and he wanted to do it, that was all.

At first light, a prisoner came to pick up the sealed case and went off to Birkenau. If the Germans asked what was inside, he need only reply that it was equipment for photographs being taken by the Identification Service. There were risks, but it had become clear to Brasse that the camp resistance was increasingly well supported.

Everything went smoothly. That evening, they brought back the case with the tripod that Walter had used to photograph prisoners, and Brasse immediately set to work developing the images, which turned out perfectly this time.

He felt encouraged by this success. It was the first time he'd participated in a resistance action since passing on the information about the counterfeit money and the enlistments in the special squads. And he'd managed to play a key role.

Over the weeks that followed, there were simpler and safer acts of resistance to be performed: falsifying documents for prisoners so they could escape from the camp.

The Germans were managing to enlist and send away more and more volunteers for their antiresistance brigades. These people were mainly the so-called asocials and German convicts, but there were also Poles who were prepared to collaborate in order to save their skins.

News was filtering in that the war was advancing toward the camp. Many lived in terror, convinced that the Germans wouldn't leave Auschwitz intact to fall into enemy hands. There was a general belief that, however things turned out, the Nazis wouldn't leave their extermination project half finished. So it was better to get out, at any cost.

The Identification Service was working overtime to process the ever-increasing number of people enlisting to leave. There were more and more secret visits from kapos and prisoners preparing to get out, all coming to be photographed. They got their SS documents but didn't appear on any official list, so it wasn't difficult to slip photos of resistance men in among all those ugly mugs. The clandestine leavers got out of the camp using the papers provided by Brasse and were then given new false documents by the resistance outside the camp.

This action was very useful to the resistance, but it involved almost no risk for Brasse and his colleagues.

At one point, someone even suggested that Brasse himself should escape, but it wasn't anyone from the resistance—he was most useful to them where he was. The offer came from a friend from Katowice, someone he'd known before the war. One morning, this friend came to have his photograph taken so he could enlist in the Wehrmacht. He looked as if he'd just won the lottery: he already had his new uniform and clearly felt that his life was about to improve considerably. The two men recognized each other straightaway.

"Wilhelm! I knew you were here somewhere!"

Brasse was embarrassed. "Hello. How are you doing?"

"How am I doing? I'm getting out, that's how I'm doing!"

"You're going to fight for them?"

His friend didn't seem offended. "I said I'm getting out. Then I'll sort myself out somehow."

Yes, Brasse had to admit there was a certain logic in that, and his friend went on.

"What about you? You're mad to stay here. In the winter, the Russians will come, but you won't be alive to see them. The Germans won't let you live. You must see that?"

Silence.

"You should leave too. As soon as you can. Enlist! Your father was Aryan. You'd have no trouble."

Brasse looked at his friend. Had Walter sent him in a desperate attempt to convince Brasse to declare himself a German?

"That's it. Keep still," he said as he carried on with the portrait.

The soldier kept his mouth shut only as long as it took to take the photograph.

"So? You need to decide. We could go together. What do you say?"

Brasse didn't hesitate, even though he couldn't look his old friend in the eye as he told him he was ashamed of him.

"No, thank you. I'm Polish, and I'll die Polish."

But his friend still didn't seem offended. He only lowered his voice a little.

"So escape, Wilhelm. Make yourself some false documents and just pretend you're going with us. Escape. You must want to do that at least?"

But Brasse was better informed about the consequences of making an escape than his companion.

"My mother and brothers are still in Żywiec. No one's laid a finger on them yet, as far as I know. But do you remember those seven who escaped from the kitchens last summer?"

"Yes, I remember. They never came back, did they? They managed it. So just imagine, you get yourself some documents—"

"Be quiet! You don't know what you're talking about!" Brasse interrupted with an edge to his voice. "Two months ago, in here, the mother of one of those men died. I'd known him before the war. The son never came back here, but they went and got her, and she didn't last long. That won't happen to my family, do you understand? And you should watch out for yours!"

The man's good humor disappeared immediately. He'd been deluding himself that he'd be able to go his own way once he escaped. Instead, he left Block 26 full of dark thoughts. Brasse was sorry, but he knew he'd been right to tell the truth. Everyone needed the truth now. There could be no more lies.

The final day, or perhaps the day of judgment, was approaching.

After that encounter, Brasse went back to his usual routine, at least superficially, but he continued to take every opportunity to do something good while there was still time.

In early September, he managed to get the first photographs he'd taken himself—of prisoners and torture—sent out of the camp. It was like putting a message in a bottle and throwing it into the sea. Was anyone interested in the pictures? Was there someone out there who could do anything for them? Was there someone who, faced with the evidence, would stop—or at least slow down—the arrival of new trains each day?

He didn't know. But he did it anyway. Photography had been his salvation until now. Perhaps it could become his weapon.

2 9

BRASSE CLUTCHED HIS STOMACH AND SHOWED ALL THE
signs of someone in increasing pain. He'd never done this—never
been ill and never pretended to be ill. The comforts of a period of
recovery in Block 20 were no better than those they already had
in Block 26, and revealing oneself to be weak and missing even
just one day of work incurred the risk of being added to the list of
prisoners who could be eliminated at any time.

But that day, he behaved as though he couldn't even stand up,
and his colleagues all believed he was really unwell.

"What's wrong?"

Trałka was shocked. For him, Brasse was a rock, steadfast in
every way, and it was unnerving to see him taken ill.

Brasse was pleased that they all believed him.

"I need to see a doctor right now," he urged. "I've got terrible stomach cramps."

As he'd predicted, it wasn't long before Walter came in. Immediately, the others told him what was happening.

"Herr Brasse is very ill," they explained worriedly.

Walter frowned but turned to Brasse quite mildly.

"What's the matter?"

Brasse looked up from the desk where he'd stayed sitting down with the air of someone determined to do his duty up until the last possible moment.

"I've got pains in my stomach, sir. Terrible cramps."

"Have you finished the work for me?"

Brasse pointed at a folder propped up in a corner. Walter opened it and examined the prints that Brasse had prepared for him extremely quickly by working deep into the night. They were a series of flyers, signed by the head of the Home Army, the biggest resistance organization in Poland. The signature and the symbols printed on all the flyers were genuine, but the text had been written by the SS. The aim was to spread false information among the Polish population: that Soviet troops had been pushed back by the Germans and had suffered grave losses; that the Polish resistance was calling on people to suspend all activities against the occupying forces until the situation improved; that negotiations were under way for an armistice between Germany and the Soviet Union, which would culminate in an agreement like the one finalized in 1939.

Walter was pleased. As always, the Political Department's orders were being carried out quickly and faultlessly. He would now send the negatives of these fake flyers into town, where they would be used to make plates. In just a few days, thousands of copies could be printed from them, creating confusion and slowing down the rebels' activities.

Brasse had followed his orders but was also aware of the serious consequences of his collaboration. It was the reason why he was clutching his stomach: he had made lots of extra copies of the flyers and stuffed them down his trousers, and now he wanted to get them to Stanisław Kłodziński, the assistant doctor who'd been his resistance contact for some time now.

He let out a low groan.

Walter looked at him. Clearly, his precious worker needed looking after.

"Don't stay here suffering, Brasse. Go to Block 20 and get yourself some medicine. Tell them I sent you. Can you get there by yourself?"

Brasse got to his feet, not too quickly, still holding his stomach.

"Yes, Herr Walter, I can, with your permission."

"Go, go. And try to be back before midday. There might be more of these things to make. I only trust you to do it."

Brasse nodded, his face showing worry at his sudden illness mixed with a continued sense of duty.

When he got to Block 20, he immediately asked for Kłodziński, but his contact wasn't there—he'd gone to tend to an urgent case in Block 14. Brasse found himself in front of a German doctor who fired questions at him.

"Are you still in pain? How long has it been hurting? How often do the cramps occur?"

Brasse gave vague answers, trying to play down his illness. He said that in the past, Kłodziński had given him medicine for a similar condition but then regretted his words—he didn't want to attract too much attention to the young Polish student.

The German doctor was growing impatient. Had Brasse been an ordinary prisoner, he'd already have been seen off with a kick, but as he was working for the Political Department and clearly wasn't someone who was starving, he must be of great value. So the doctor resisted the temptation to throw him out.

"Forget about Kłodziński, I'll examine you. Undress and lie down here." He pointed to a bed covered in a grimy sheet. "I need to find out if something serious is causing the pain."

Brasse turned pale.

"Do I... Do I have to undress?"

"Of course you do! What's the matter? Hurry up!"

There were several witnesses in the room. Another doctor, some nurses, and even a few patients had already turned to look at them.

"I—I—" Brasse stammered. "I've never... I don't want to..."

The doctor was obviously irritated, but then his face lit up with a sudden intuition. He moved closer to Brasse and lowered his voice.

"You're Jewish, and you've never admitted it. Isn't that right?"

Brasse nodded vigorously. "Yes. I beg you. I—I'm an indispensable collaborator for Herr Walter. I've worked at the Erkennungsdienst for four years. I've always followed orders…"

"Calm down. I'll just do a quick examination," the doctor said, trying to reassure him.

But Brasse stepped back and raised his voice in order to attract even more attention.

"But what about the others? We're not alone, Doctor!"

He took another step backward toward the exit. The doctor looked around and was greeted by several curious glances. He turned back to Brasse…but the photographer was gone.

He'd left and was now walking quickly back to his block. He was still trembling with fear. He had to admit that he wasn't up to much as a resistance operative. He forced himself to calm down, to control his thoughts. He couldn't go straight back to Block 20, but he could hang around for as long as the excuse of being ill would mean his superiors in the Identification Service wouldn't miss him. He stopped. Yes, he could do that. He must simply avoid drawing attention to himself.

He retraced his steps and, when he was close to the hospital block, began to look around while still trying to look as though he were carrying out an important errand. If a guard or a kapo interrogated him, he could just tell them who he was and say he needed to see a doctor.

He carried on walking, never moving far from the block where, sooner or later, Kłodziński would surely reappear.

The men he encountered were too tired and weak to wonder about him, and indeed they barely even looked at him. Work teams filed past without much conviction, dragging their feet. After the first half hour or so, Brasse began to realize that the rhythm of the usual camp activities had slowed down. It was as though everyone was waiting for new orders, and in the meantime, the surveillance and abuse of prisoners had been temporarily suspended.

It must be an illusion, he told himself. And he didn't once stop looking over his shoulder and trying as best he could to avoid being observed.

Finally, he glimpsed the Polish assistant doctor walking toward Block 20. Luckily, he had a bag with him. Slowly, without showing that he'd finally found the man who could get him out of a difficult situation, Brasse moved toward Kłodziński, who saw him and realized immediately that something was up. He, too, avoided hurrying or changing direction.

When they met, it was as if by chance.

"I've got fake resistance flyers," Brasse said, still clutching his stomach.

"Fake flyers? What do they say?"

"That the war's going well for the Germans. In particular, that the Russians are prepared to sign an agreement with them."

Kłodziński smiled confidently. "The SS are firing their last few bullets. I don't know who on earth would believe such an obvious lie."

"Why? It doesn't seem so unbelievable to me."

After he'd risked so much to pass on the information, Brasse was almost offended that Kłodziński wasn't taking this more seriously.

The doctor's face took on a grave expression. He looked around, and not seeing anyone dangerous, he went up to Brasse and put down his bag. He lifted one side of the prisoner's jacket and began to press on his stomach, as though he were carrying out an impromptu examination. At the same time, still looking around him, he began to speak.

"It's over, Brasse. There won't be an agreement between the Russians and the Germans. The Russians are advancing. They'll be here soon. It'll be a matter of weeks. We won't spend another winter in the camp. They'll transfer us somewhere else. But the Russians won't stop here. They might go all the way to Berlin. So they're not interested in dividing up the country. If anything, they want to take back the whole of Poland this time. We might need to fight them, too, when the Germans have gone. If we manage to save our own skins, that is."

This confused speech, fragments of news mixed with guesswork and perhaps with propaganda, left Brasse stunned, openmouthed. Anybody who saw the pair of them there would have no doubts that the prisoner being examined really was ill.

A moment later, the flyers were quickly slipped into the bag lying open on the ground, and Kłodziński closed it. Then he straightened up and sent Brasse on his way with a pat on the back.

"I'll take care of the flyers. Thank you. We won't forget it. If the Germans make more, try to get them to me. These will be out of the camp by this evening and in Warsaw in a couple of days. Your stomach is cured. Just try not to get indigestion in Block 25!"

He was lighthearted enough to joke, and Brasse could see that his good humor was genuine, which disconcerted him even more than the doctor's words and promises. They took leave of one another, and the photographer, having made a miraculous recovery, walked back to the laboratory.

Walter was waiting for him on the threshold, his uniform impeccable, his arms crossed, looking like a boss surveying his employees to make sure they weren't causing trouble. While he was still some distance away, Brasse signaled to Walter that all was well.

Seeing the Hauptscharführer's satisfied expression and knowing how absorbed he was in his important mission, it was impossible to take Kłodziński's claims seriously. It was already midautumn, and yet the doctor had talked of transferral, perhaps even freedom, within a few weeks, before the winter. Incredible!

But Kłodziński was in touch with the world outside the camp…

Walter was solicitous. "Everything all right?"

"Everything's all right," Brasse confirmed.

He almost stood at attention, and he realized that after all these years of service, the camp was in his blood, a thought that came as a revelation. Walter was ready to give him more orders, and he was ready to obey them, because that was what he was used to doing. And this, in some absurd way, reassured him, gave him familiar landmarks to which he could always return. All the rest was the unknown. It was a future that he couldn't conceive of, because thinking about the future was something he'd denied himself for too long.

"I've got more flyers to be prepared," Walter said.

It was clear that brandishing the weapon of propaganda gave the officer renewed certainty of Germany's imminent victory. Did he really believe in it? It was impossible to say. Impossible to understand, yet again, where the dream ended and reality began.

Brasse shivered with cold and hurried inside.

"I'll get to work straightaway, Herr Hauptscharführer."

As soon as he was inside, he was warm again. He knew he wouldn't stop collaborating with the resistance, but in the meantime, he was also ready for his fifth winter in the camp.

30

It was December now. December 1944. Perhaps there had been good reasons why, three or four months ago, the camp resistance had thought that the war would soon be over, that the Russians were knocking at the door, and that they would liberate Auschwitz before the winter. But the weeks passed without change, and the Germans carried on as though they had all the time in the world at their disposal. Time to murder the Jews and political prisoners who kept on arriving in droves; time to make sure that prisoners selected for new medical experiments—twin children or girls with eyes of two different colors—were securely shut up in the basements of the blocks assigned to them…and time to kill Oberkapo Rudolf Friemel, the young husband of Margarita Ferrer. Their extraordinary day of celebration, which Brasse had immortalized with the best wedding photos that could be produced in the camp, had been nearly a year ago.

He and Friemel had become friends. This Austrian man, a Communist and longtime enemy of Fascism and Hitler, held an influential position in the camp and had always done much more for the others there than Brasse could ever have hoped to do. Friemel had always been willing to find a safe job for a desperate prisoner in his workshop, where they repaired motor vehicles. He'd also been incredibly active in supporting the resistance and had contacts outside the camp that Brasse would never have thought possible—groups of active rebels very close to Auschwitz.

Friemel must have hoped they would help him, or he would never have tried to escape as he did, with another Austrian and a Pole. Brasse had never had the chance to talk to him about his plans for this attempt. If he had, he would probably have tried to dissuade him. He would have told him to be patient, to wait longer. After all, if the order came to evacuate the camp and to eliminate as many prisoners as possible, Friemel's help would have been invaluable to the fleeing Germans. He would have had a far greater chance of survival than so many other wretches who were by now on the brink of collapse—shadows of men who weighed seventy pounds and couldn't even get up from their bunks. The Germans were now taking some of these men away while they were still alive but comatose from hunger and thirst. They were burning them as they were, in great heaps or stuffed into the crematorium ovens.

But Friemel hadn't been able to wait any longer.

Had he escaped because he'd discovered something that others didn't know? Had he learned that the Germans were planning to bomb the camp, burn it, or destroy it somehow with all the prisoners still inside? Everyone wondered, including Brasse himself. They were painful questions to which no one had an answer.

They hanged Friemel on December 30, along with the other Austrian and the Pole. Witnesses to the hanging reported that, just before the execution, Friemel had shouted, "Long live Austria! Long live Austria! Long live freedom!"

The Pole, too, had shouted, "Long live Poland!"

Even at the moment of his death, then, Friemel had thought of his country, of liberty, and of the future of humanity. He hadn't thought of his wife and son. Or perhaps he'd kept that thought, the most precious one, to himself. Margarita had come all the way to Auschwitz to marry him, so she'd seen the camp. Even though it had been a day of celebration and the groom and Brasse, as their witness, had worn civilian clothes, she must have understood the horror of the place where the man she loved was imprisoned.

In Auschwitz, for one night, they had loved one another.

Brasse knew, and if he survived, he would shout it out loud: even in Auschwitz, there had been love. Every form of love: love between a man and a woman, self-sacrifice for another prisoner, sincere and loyal friendship, and love of one's country. The hope of a better world for everyone.

The Erkennungsdienst had a new colleague in the laboratory, Bronisław Jureczek. Brasse had done everything he could to help him, and now here he was. Once he had joined their number, thought Brasse, Jureczek must have hoped that he was safe, but now he was discovering that nobody was ever safe in the inferno of the camp.

Brasse tormented himself over Friemel's death. His friend had fought for a better world and had succeeded in making even Auschwitz a slightly better place, but now he was dead. Would his son, far away, fare any better?

Brasse found the pictures of the wedding and the family portrait he'd taken. In secret, he looked at the picture of the three of them for a long time. Margarita was smiling at little Edi. Rudolf, also smiling, was looking straight at the camera, as if to give courage to whoever was looking at him. Edi was the only one not smiling: he was looking beyond the camera with a worried expression, as though he wasn't taken in by his parents' smiles. An innocent who knew the truth. His eyes said that, even though everyone had forced themselves to celebrate at the wedding, he expected the worst. They said, *They'll kill my daddy here. And Mummy won't ever smile again.*

Now that Rudolf was dead, that photograph had become irrevocably, irremediably sad.

Brasse had already made up his mind that this picture, too,

must be saved. He couldn't allow Rudolf—a good man who could have thought only of himself but instead decided to help others—to disappear forever, as though he had never existed.

Edi would have the picture of his handsome father. One day, he would look at the kind face of that honest man, and in his smile, he would find the strength to stand up to anything and everyone.

Brasse thumbed the photograph, checked the negative was still intact, and put them both carefully back into their folder. He would place it alongside the others, which contained thousands and thousands of images of men and women who had really existed.

They were depending on him.

I'm ready, he said to himself.

There was nothing more to do but wait for the time to come.

3 1

"This one's ready too, Herr Hauptscharführer."

Brasse and Jureczek showed Walter the heavy wooden case prepared according to his orders and sealed so there could be no doubt as to the secrecy of its contents. They exchanged a brief glance, but their faces remained impassive. They had stuffed it full of all the photographs, negatives, and rolls of film that recorded the elimination of the Russian prisoners of war years earlier. Most of this kind of material was sent outside the camp to be developed, but Walter himself, who'd produced it all, had spent the last few days insisting worriedly that no trace should remain of this crime. The Germans clearly feared the arrival of the Russians and were getting rid of any evidence directly related to them as quickly as they could.

Brasse was disgusted. His superiors didn't seem at all troubled by the thousands of photographs of Jewish or Polish prisoners or those from other occupied countries. Nor were they concerned about the pictures of Mengele's experiments or all the negatives of portraits of SS officers. At least they weren't worried yet.

The persecutors seemed to fear only the vengeance of those forces stronger than themselves: the soon-to-be victors. No one seemed to care about the civilian victims carried off up the crematorium chimneys and borne away by the wind or to be demanding justice for them. The Nazis had considered millions of people to be nonentities, abandoned by God and men, and had treated them accordingly, convinced of their complete impunity. And they were still doing it.

It was the photographs of these innocents, so easily forgotten, that Brasse and his colleagues now watched over in Block 26.

Walter didn't bother to check the contents of the case. He trusted his subordinates blindly, especially Brasse, his obedient servant for four years. The Hauptscharführer summoned two SS men, who lifted up the precious burden and looked at him inquiringly.

"That's to go with the rest of the things from the Political Department being sent away today," he explained.

Pretending to be busy with his usual tasks, Brasse strained to hear where all the material was being sent, but it was impossible.

The calendar hanging from the wall announced that it was January 15, 1945. For almost all the prisoners in the camp, life was carrying on as usual: the usual duties, the usual killing of the weakest, the usual distribution of tiny rations. But at the Erkennungsdienst, there was no longer any doubt that the Russians were coming soon.

Soon but not immediately. Or at least that was what they thought.

Evening fell. The kommando went out for the evening roll call, lining up in the cold, shifting their toes in their broken shoes to stop them freezing. They all answered the call, watched closely by the SS, who were still calm and in charge of the situation.

Then, just after the order had come to disperse, Brasse was as surprised as everyone else to hear the roar of an engine approaching the square. They all turned toward the sound and saw a figure astride a motorbike. It was Walter. He careened through the ranks of prisoners, who scattered to make room for him. Skidding on the frozen ground, he came to a stop next to Brasse.

"Brasse!" he shouted over the sound of the engine. "The Russians are coming!"

The photographer looked around. All the other prisoners had made off as quickly as they could, fearing that Walter wanted to take his anger out on someone at random. None of them heard his agitated outburst.

In any case, Walter's mind was on other things. He was panicking, as though a column of enemy soldiers had already entered the camp.

"Burn all the photographs, all the documents, everything! Everything! Do it now!"

Brasse stood rooted to the spot.

It was happening, just like that, without warning.

Walter didn't hang around waiting for a reply. He already had his foot on the accelerator, ready to drive past Brasse and flee.

Before speeding off, he bellowed into Brasse's ear, "I'll come back tomorrow morning to make sure everything's gone. Do you understand?"

Brasse nodded, and Walter raced off into the freezing darkness.

A few moments later, there was complete silence. The last few prisoners disappeared this way and that behind the barracks buildings. Only Jureczek had stopped several feet away and was looking at him, full of curiosity.

Brasse shook himself, went over to his colleague, and told him about the order he'd just received.

"Let's go," he said. "We need to work quickly!"

They ran to Block 26, rushed inside, and immediately began to empty the cupboards, throwing packets of negatives and rolls of film on to the table pell-mell. Walter had told them to burn everything. Brasse glanced at the stove—their precious, vital companion on the terrible winter days. The fire was only ever lit during the day, to save wood, but it was evening now. He opened it up and saw that it contained only ashes and a few glowing embers.

The photographer didn't hesitate. He could almost feel Walter's eyes boring into his back, but a voice inside him, a voice that had been wanting to speak for a long time, began to make itself heard. It followed the rhythm of his heavy breathing, becoming more and more like the ticking of a bomb that becomes louder and louder as the moment of explosion creeps closer.

Now was his chance to act. To do what he wanted to do. He hadn't made any plans, but now fate was helping him along.

He immediately knew what he had to do. "Inside!" he ordered Jureczek. "Everything inside!"

They crammed packets and packets of negatives into the stove. One, two, three… Carrying on until there was no more space. Jureczek followed the order but glanced wide-eyed at Brasse as he did so.

"But, Wilhelm, there are far too many if we put them all in! And it isn't lit! We need to find some gasoline. Let's ask the SS. They'll give us some."

Brasse fixed his companion with a determined look in his eyes.

"Carry on! We only need to show that we tried to follow the order. Carry on!"

The films wouldn't burn. The heat caused a few marks to appear on them here and there, and they were dirtied by the ash, but nothing more than that.

"This stuff isn't flammable!" said Jureczek.

Perhaps he hadn't known that, or perhaps he'd forgotten, but now the poor boy was really frightened.

Brasse took no notice. He looked quickly at the hundreds of pictures piled on the table. Men, women, and children intended for medical experiments, alongside the neat, clean faces of uniformed

SS men. A tide of memories broke over him in an instant. Years of imprisonment and servitude passed before his eyes. There they all were, right in front of him. He realized he could tell the story behind every single picture, and this awareness filled him with an energy and resolve he'd never felt before.

I might die tomorrow morning, he thought, *but these people won't. They won't!*

Without a second's hesitation, he rushed to the stove. With great urgency, he began to pull out everything they'd just piled into it.

Jureczek stepped back in horror.

"What are you doing?" he cried. "Wilhelm, what are you doing?"

Brasse smiled at him with wild excitement. "Go. Go away now. I'll do this. I was the one who was given the order!"

As he spoke, he blew on the rolls of film, brushing off the hot ash with his fingers.

"I'll answer to Walter tomorrow morning," he said, trying to calm himself. "Don't you see? The heat has left marks on them. As soon as he regains his senses, that bastard will understand that it was impossible for me to destroy anything. Even he knows that these things don't burn. Tomorrow morning, he'll come to his senses and remember that."

But Jureczek didn't leave. He stood there, still staring at his boss, who had now begun to wash the ash off the negatives with water. Then, mechanically, gradually understanding what was going on, he, too, began to clean the images. As they worked, their hearts nearly stopped twice: a vehicle drove past the block, then another one. But they didn't slow down.

Now Brasse had started to put everything back in order. He was even replacing the negatives in their packets, but Jureczek stopped him.

"No, don't do that! Listen, let's spread the pictures around the lab. We'll mess them all up, hide them… Then, if we have to leave the camp in a hurry, no one will have time to pick them all up and take them!"

Brasse thanked the boy with a look: he'd understood and wanted to help. And it was a good idea.

They scattered negatives, rolls of film, and printed pictures all around the room: on and underneath tables, behind furniture, even in the secret place where they'd always hidden food and cigarettes. It looked for all the world as though they'd been seized with panic and turned everything upside down in their desperate attempt to destroy it all.

When it was done, they found themselves standing there, silent. And afraid.

"Tomorrow morning, Walter will put a bullet through our heads," Jureczek said with certainty, as though he were pronouncing his own death sentence.

Brasse only smiled. He was calm, even serene.

"No. Tomorrow morning, I'll be the only one here. Walter is terrified, and if he wants to take it out on someone, that person will be me. But all he'll be able to do is try again to make me succeed in what we failed to do this evening. Until then, the pictures are safe. And that's all that counts, you see, right up to the very end!"

They locked up the studio, but as they were leaving, Brasse had a second thought.

"We should barricade the door of the lab with chairs and furniture. I'll say I thought the Russians were about to arrive and that was the only way to delay them... In fact, it'll be Walter who'll have no time to waste, and he'll have to leave everything as it is."

They turned back and blocked the door, transforming the laboratory into a sealed cell, with its treasury of the living and the dead waiting to be seen by new eyes.

Finally, panting with cold and fear, Brasse and Jureczek went back to Block 25.

The others looked at them questioningly. No one could sleep. The kommando talked all night, discussing Walter's order, his fear, his haste. Their uncertainty made the night seem interminable. They had never felt so trapped. Several times, they looked outside, defying the curfew, and saw that the German guard was present and alert, as always. They couldn't understand why Walter had been so afraid.

They waited anxiously, jumping to their feet every time they heard—or thought they heard—shots or distant rumbles. Was it an engine? A truck? A motorbike? A plane?

Suddenly, they heard a shout in the darkness: "Halt!" Then came a shot and dogs barking. Somebody hadn't been able to stand the tension and had tried to escape.

Then silence again. Seconds, minutes, hours. It felt as if morning would never come. It seemed to Brasse, tortured by the wait and plagued by his own desperate actions, that perhaps the end of the camp, with all its unthinkable horrors, was actually the end of the world.

Finally, it began to grow light, and the morning wake-up call, the same one that had sounded every morning for years, echoed across the camp. Today, its sound struck fear in them.

As they made their way outside, they saw the other prisoners coming out for roll call, looking around cautiously. Few had slept.

Everyone lined up and answered the call.

Then Brasse, who had managed to convince Jureczek and the others to return to Block 25, made his way to the Erkennungsdienst alone. He arrived at Block 26 just like he did every morning, but instead of going inside, he sat on the steps up to the entrance. The morning was very cold, but he no longer felt it. He was ready to die in front of this door that held, sealed behind it, a little shrine of memories.

The camp was waking up. Orders rang through the air, barked out by kapos determined to remind their prisoners that Auschwitz was still Auschwitz, and they shouldn't believe the rumors of fleeing officials.

The minutes passed. Neither Walter nor his underling Hofmann were anywhere to be seen.

Half an hour went by. Brasse stayed there, his mind empty of thoughts. By now, he had even stopped imagining the scenario of Walter arriving out of breath, perhaps with a couple of SS officers, and asking him if he'd destroyed everything, then asking to go inside and seeing photos strewn around and negatives barely touched by fire. And then growing furious and pulling out his pistol…

He'd stopped thinking about it since the moment he had realized that, whatever happened, he wouldn't say anything, right up to the end. He wouldn't answer any questions, wouldn't whisper any excuses. His silence would be his farewell to the world. *I'm not saying anything, Herr Hauptscharführer. I won't ever say anything, but for me, these thousands of photographs will speak forever!*

An SS man walked past, scowling, caught up in his own thoughts. He didn't take any notice of Brasse, didn't even seem to see him.

A pale sun began to shine.

Brasse waited all morning, gesturing at his colleagues to go away on the several occasions when they peered timidly around the corner of Block 25 to see how things were going.

Walter didn't come. Nobody came.

The Identification Service was no more. The whole Political Department had probably fled.

Once midday had passed, the photographer got to his feet and returned to his companions. He left the studio closed and sealed shut and joined the others to wait for orders.

None of them ever went back into the laboratory where they'd worked for years. Over the next few days, they were forced to take part in the evacuation operation, amid shouts and confusion, contradictory orders and terrible threats. No longer set apart from the other prisoners, they were placed with a group made up of those who were still in a fit state to march.

They departed from Auschwitz on the morning of January 21, 1945. Filing out through the main gates, they left the camp, not knowing where they would end up.

Marching alongside the others, Brasse managed one last glance back at Block 26, still all shut up.

It was a look of farewell. He hoped the Russians would make good use of the memorial that he had risked his life to entrust to them and to the world.

He took only one photograph with him: his portrait of Baśka.

He was walking toward life and freedom. Perhaps.

And perhaps, in some faraway camp, she was doing the same thing.

EPILOGUE

"WHERE ARE YOU GOING?"

The Russian soldier was carrying out his duties without much enthusiasm. He, like everyone else, probably didn't understand why everyone still had to be on alert now that Germany had surrendered, just in case a new enemy was hiding among the crowds of ordinary people. He held out his hand to check the papers of the young man who'd just gotten off the bus on one of the first routes to have been restored since the war.

Brasse's documents had been provided by the Americans and the Red Cross. The Red Cross certificate said that he had registered as a Polish citizen in Katowice in July 1945 and that he'd been in Mauthausen.

As the soldier read the name of the Austrian town, he looked up and scrutinized the man in front of him with increased respect.

Mauthausen's reputation as one of the most dreaded concentration camps was growing.

Brasse knew what was going through the soldier's mind, and it was a familiar experience. He was thankful that the name Auschwitz didn't appear on his papers. Otherwise, he would have had to answer an endless series of curious, incredulous questions about his experiences and how he'd managed to survive.

Without giving the soldier time to think, he answered the question straightaway.

"I'm going to Kraków—to the suburbs. I'm looking for someone..."

Over the soldier's shoulders, Brasse could see the city in the distance.

"Have you got relatives there?" the soldier asked, returning Brasse's papers and signaling to the soldiers at the checkpoint to allow the civilian back on the bus.

"No, my family are all in Żywiec. That's where I live. I'm going to visit someone who...who I knew during the war."

"Well, off you go, and good luck."

Brasse received the good wishes with a polite smile. He'd need that luck.

When the bus, carrying only those passengers who'd passed through the checkpoint, stopped in the town center, he got off and began walking through the streets of the town, enjoying the sights of this historic Polish city that had suffered almost no damage during the war. It was one of the few.

He could have reached his destination very quickly if he'd wanted. He knew that in these weeks so soon after the end of the war, even though people on the streets were caught up in the worries and anxieties of a population starting from scratch, they still reacted kindly to strangers who might be wandering around searching for relatives or who were returning to less fortunate areas only to find their houses destroyed, irreparably damaged, or empty after being looted by other desperate people.

Still, he preferred to prolong his own wanderings. He wanted to reach his destination of course, but he was also afraid of doing so, although he couldn't have said why.

In his pocket, along with his papers and the small amount of money his mother had given him, was a piece of card bearing an address and a photograph.

Baśka's portrait.

Kraków wasn't far from Żywiec. She'd given him the address during one of their meetings in the camp. He could only hope that she was still alive, but he'd never doubted that as soon as he was free, he would go straight to her house.

He'd imagined their reunion a thousand times. A moment full of emotion, unhoped-for kisses, tears of relief, and plans for a future, the very thought of which made his soul want to burst.

Midday came. He spent a few pennies on some black bread and salami and ate his meal sitting on a bench in a beautiful park. He was hungry, and everything around him spoke to him of peace, security, and ordinary life, but his stomach was suffering from the tension, the anticipation of a meeting with reality that could be put off no longer.

He threw his last crumbs of bread to the pigeons. This was a luxury that would have been unimaginable even three months earlier: to be so rich and so sure of where his next meal was coming from that he could afford to feed the birds.

That's it, he said to himself. *Time to go.*

He got to his feet, took a deep breath, and set off to ask directions toward the address he held in his hand.

An hour later, he found himself standing in a suburban district in front of a house that looked modest but was at least intact. Three stone steps led up to a green door that needed a new coat of varnish.

There were several names written next to the door, and his heart leaped to see that one of them was Tytoniak. Baśka was short for Stefańska, as he already knew, and he also knew that Stefańska was the name she had given in the camp instead of her real one: Anna. So she was Anna Tytoniak. Now, if she was alive, should he use that name when he spoke to her?

He didn't stop to think. He didn't think about anything else.

He knocked. Waited. Then he knocked louder. He felt as though he were making enough noise to attract the attention of the whole street, but it was just his imagination; people kept on walking without even glancing at him.

He knocked for a third time.

He heard footsteps. The door opened, and she appeared.

"Wilhelm!"

As she said his name, she covered her mouth with her hands. Her eyes widened. She was surprised. No, afraid.

He smiled uncertainly. Her appearance and her reaction had unbalanced him. She was extremely thin and pale and was wearing an old faded dress. Her hair was streaked with white and pulled back in a short ponytail. It was Baśka, but it was as though years had passed since they'd last met.

"May I...?"

She nodded and let him in. They stood looking at each other shyly in the hallway. He smiled again, trying to seem natural, but she dropped her eyes and led him along a straight, narrow corridor.

They sat down in a clean, dimly lit sitting room—the best room in the house, perhaps. Brasse felt a heavy silence all around them.

Was there nobody else there? Was she alone?

He couldn't bring himself to ask questions. He kept on looking at her and smiling, but something in her manner made his courage drain away.

Baśka was sitting down, but she was perched on the very edge of her chair, her back stiff and straight. She was still staring at him with something like fear in her eyes, and she kept touching her hair, almost as if she was trying to hide it rather than tidy it.

"Why have you come?" she whispered.

It was a fair question. But it was the wrong question. He felt this immediately and suddenly seemed to see inside her. *Was there really*, he thought to himself all of a sudden, *anything to explain?* They were alive, that was all. They were alive, and they could see each other. He had come to her as soon as he could…

Stupidly, in his confusion, he answered with another question.

"What did you say?"

She seemed annoyed.

"Why have you come?"

Should he get up and embrace her? He didn't know what to do, but he did know that he couldn't possibly begin to explain what he'd done and how he felt. But she was still silent and immobile, looking at him as though from a long way away.

He sighed. Putting his hand in his pocket, he took out the portrait and handed it to her.

"I wanted to give you this."

He had dreamed that he would be performing an act of love by showing the proof of his devotion to her, this sign of the vivid and tender memory of her that had survived within him during so many months of horror. But as he said the words and made the gesture, as the image, passing from one hand to another, crossed the little room, he felt as though he were falling into a great ravine. A loud voice inside him shouted that this was wrong, he'd gotten it all wrong. She was alive, yes, but that meant he was bringing death and fear back to her. And the photograph, the photograph…

Too late.

Baśka took the picture and stared at it. She didn't say anything for a long time.

Then she tore it up. Into two, into four, then a hundred pieces, which she let fall to the ground.

"I don't like myself in this picture," she said. But she didn't say it to apologize for what she'd done. It was the truth, that was all.

Then she went back to staring at him silently, showing no emotion.

He lowered his eyes, and they rested on the fragments of his memory scattered over the scrupulously clean old carpet.

Later, walking quickly alone through the beautiful town that was coming back to life, Brasse remembered a saying that his uncle Lech had taught him: "Always remember that neither the good Lord nor a photographer can ever make a woman completely happy."

A True Story

THE PROTAGONISTS

Wilhelm Brasse was born on December 3, 1917, in the town of Żywiec, which was then part of the Austro-Hungarian Empire and became Polish after the First World War. His father's family was Austrian, and his mother was Polish.

In the 1930s, Brasse learned the art of photography in Katowice, where his uncle ran a studio. Katowice, in Polish Silesia, was then a rich, cosmopolitan city where Germans, Jews, and Poles all lived together.

In 1939, after Germany invaded Poland, the young Brasse was interrogated several times by the SS. He refused to swear loyalty to Hitler and enlist in the Wehrmacht, insisting that he felt himself to be Polish, a feeling initially inspired in him by his mother. He tried to escape to Hungary, wanting to join the Free

Polish Army in France, but was captured at the border in late March 1940. Imprisoned for five months—first at Sanok and then Tarnów—he still refused to join the Nazis. On August 31, 1940, he was deported to Auschwitz, where he was given the number 3444 and classified as a political prisoner.

Of the 438 people who arrived with him, most died during their first few weeks in the camp.

Brasse endured terrible suffering during his first months in Auschwitz. He was forced to carry out extremely hard labor in inhumane conditions, including constructing the road between the station and the crematorium and knocking down nearby Polish-owned houses that had been requisitioned as the camp expanded. He also had to transport corpses from the camp hospital to the crematorium. In the middle of the winter of 1940–41, he managed to get a job in the kitchens, where he carried tubs full of potatoes to the ovens. Finally, in February 1941, he was summoned to the Political Department, where the Germans assigned him to work at the Erkennungsdienst, Auschwitz's Identification Service. Brasse was saved by his knowledge of photography, acquired during his teenage years, and the fact that he spoke fluent German. This book focuses on his experiences in the Identification Service.

In January 1945, as the Red Army approached, Auschwitz was abandoned, and the Erkennungsdienst ceased to exist. According to his own estimates, Brasse took between forty thousand and fifty thousand photographs during his four years of uninterrupted work at the Identification Service.

As the Germans were abandoning Auschwitz, Brasse risked his life to save a large number of the pictures—some taken by him and others taken by the SS—from being destroyed. We owe the survival of vital sources of knowledge and memory about horrors perpetrated by the Nazis to him.

Brasse was then taken to the Ebensee camp, a subcamp of Mauthausen, in Austria, and he was liberated from there by American soldiers at the beginning of May 1945.

Brasse, who was still only twenty-seven, returned to Żywiec and was reunited with his family: his parents and five brothers had all survived the war. Needing to rebuild a life for himself, Brasse thought of pursuing his profession as a photographer, but when he held a camera in his hands again, he realized he couldn't do it. Every time he looked through the viewfinder, he saw the dead of Auschwitz. Ghosts of the Nazis' victims would be standing there next to the boys and girls having their photographs taken in his studio in Żywiec.

Knowing it was impossible for him to escape such a terrible past, Brasse put down his camera and never took it up again. He started a business and led a peaceful life. He married and had two children and five grandchildren. He helped create the Auschwitz-Birkenau State Museum and spent many years educating young people, especially Germans, about the Holocaust. He died peacefully in his hometown of Żywiec on October 23, 2012.

In January 1945, Brasse's immediate superior in the Erkennungsdienst, SS Hauptscharführer Bernhard Walter, was transferred to the Mittelbau-Dora concentration camp in Thuringia, where the Germans were building V-2 missiles. Captured after the war and put on trial, he was given a short sentence of three years in prison.

Ernst Hofmann, an SS officer and Walter's right-hand man at the Identification Service, was tried after the war and condemned to life in prison.

Maximilian Grabner, Walter's superior who ran the Political Department, was condemned to death after the war and executed.

Hauptsturmführer **Hans Aumeier**, who tried to convince Brasse to enlist in the Wehrmacht toward the end of the war, worked in several concentration camps. After the war, he was condemned to death and executed.

Karl Fritzsch, the deputy camp commandant who welcomed Brasse and his fellow prisoners to Auschwitz by predicting their imminent deaths, died in early 1945 fighting the Russians on the front line.

Dr. Friedrich Karl Hermann Entress, who had an interest in tattoos, was condemned to death after the war and executed.

Dr. Josef Mengele, who was responsible for the most horrific medical experiments on Auschwitz prisoners, was never captured or brought to justice. After the war, he fled to South America, where he died in 1979.

Dr. Eduard Wirths, who was always on the lookout for women with eyes of different colors, gave himself up to the British at the end of the war and committed suicide.

Dr. Carl Clauberg, who ordered Brasse to photograph gynecological experiments, was never arrested and died without ever being brought to trial.

Dr. Maximilian Samuel, a German Jew imprisoned in Auschwitz who was forced to help Clauberg or be killed himself, died in the camp before it was liberated.

Dr. Johann Paul Kremer, for whom Brasse photographed the livers of murdered Jews, was condemned to death in 1947. The sentence was commuted to life imprisonment, and Kremer was freed in 1960.

SOURCES

The direct sources of this book are *The Portraitist*, a 2005 Polish television documentary featuring a long interview with Wilhelm Brasse, and *Wilhelm Brasse: Photographer 3444, Auschwitz*

1940–1945, a book containing Brasse's direct accounts of all the episodes narrated here. It was published in English in 2012 by Sussex Academic Press.

There are innumerable general sources about the Holocaust during the Second World War and about Auschwitz itself. We recommend three texts for their completeness and importance.

The first is *The Destruction of the European Jews* by historian Raul Hilberg, first published in 1963 and republished several times since.

The second is *Commandant of Auschwitz* by Rudolf Höss, who was the camp commandant for several years. Höss wrote his memoir before being hanged by the Poles in 1947.

The third text is *Night* by Elie Wiesel, who survived Auschwitz, Buna, and Buchenwald. His account was first published in the 1950s.

A Note on the Text

In 2011, our Italian publisher, Piemme, asked us to seek out a previously untold story relating to the tragedy of the Second World War concentration camps that we could research and bring to a wider audience for the first time.

We began to explore several different accounts of heroes who had endangered their own lives to defend Jewish families and other victims of political persecution in Italy and Europe as a whole. We discovered several remarkable individuals who fit this profile but weren't able to gather quite enough evidence to reconstruct their stories in sufficient detail.

Just as we were about to give up, Maurizio discovered the briefest of press agency reports on the website of the Italian newspaper *La Stampa*. "The photographer of Auschwitz, Wilhelm Brasse, has died in Kraków," it read.

The report was so short that it was clear to us that nobody at the newspaper had any idea who this person had been. We were immediately curious. Who was this man? To what exactly did the phrase "the photographer of Auschwitz" allude? We found very little written about Wilhelm Brasse online; he'd clearly remained silent about his role in the history of Auschwitz for a long time, and we wanted to find out why.

We discovered that two years earlier (more than sixty years after the camp was liberated), Brasse had agreed to be interviewed by the BBC for a documentary they were making about him. We obtained the recording of this interview, in which the ex-prisoner (who was held at Auschwitz for five long years) talked about a series of photographs he had produced and recalled the circumstances in which each one had been taken.

With the help of the Consulate General of Poland in Milan, we traced Brasse's two children: his daughter lives in Kraków, and his son is a doctor who, at that time, was working in China. We contacted and interviewed them both about their father's memories of his years in the camp. Then we got in touch with the Auschwitz-Birkenau State Museum and Yad Vashem—the World Holocaust Remembrance Center in Jerusalem—and obtained additional photographs and information about the subjects of Brasse's pictures.

Our next step was to fill out the context of the photographer's story, consulting extensive documentation recommended by writers and historians who have studied life in the camp as well as first-person accounts. Once we'd reached the point where we could begin to tell Brasse's story in detail, we started to construct this book, basing it—as the BBC documentary before us had done—on the "story" told by those images taken by the prisoner-photographer: from the thousands of identity photographs of new arrivals at the camp to portraits of SS officers, from printed postcards sent from Auschwitz (showing pretty flowers, for example) to the horrifying records of experiments carried out on prisoners.*

Brasse's story ends with an unsatisfactory meeting with Baśka. The whole episode, including the final sentence, was a story that Brasse himself told. The final sentence, Brasse's afterthought about a saying his uncle used, seems to be inappropriate. The story of Brasse's experiences at Auschwitz is of much greater consequence than what a man needs to do in order to "make a woman completely happy."

However, this concluding thought of Brasse's is of great psychological interest, an example of how the wounds suffered in the concentration camp environment could affect the very souls of the protagonists. His closing thought might sound strange or even absurd to us. It is not what we expect Brasse to be thinking at this poignant moment. However, it reveals the deep personal alienation of someone who has experienced the brutal inhumanity of Auschwitz. As soon as we are able to understand that this

---

* The archives of these experiments are held in Yad Vashem. We received kind permission to consult but not publish them, out of respect for the victims and their families.

strangeness is part of that alienation, then we move closer to understanding the complicated feelings of the protagonists in a story like this.

It is a story that has been read in many countries—the Netherlands, Germany, Japan, and China among them—and which has now been translated into English. Such international interest, we believe, is a result of the originality and fullness of the book's depiction of Wilhelm Brasse and his extraordinary human experience. It is a story that needs to live on.

Reading Group Guide

1. Before reading, how familiar were you with the atrocities committed in Auschwitz and other concentration camps during WWII? What did you learn throughout the book?

2. Do you think Wilhelm Brasse had a choice to become the camp photographer? Would it have been possible for him to refuse?

3. Why does Brasse avoid other prisoners so desperately? What are the consequences of his aggressive incuriosity, and how does he handle it when he learns about the camp anyway?

4. Brasse originally takes a dim view of any attempts to

communicate with the outside world. How does his opinion develop over the course of the book?

5. What was Walter's goal in showing Brasse the film of the Russians? What did he actually accomplish?

6. Discuss the risks involved when Brasse accepts personal jobs for people like Schobeck, who asks Brasse to enlarge his family portraits. Why does Brasse take the chance of negotiating?

7. Brasse worries about losing his sense of identity in the process of making a pact with the Germans. Sometimes, as in the case of the twins that Mengele sends, he has others print the pictures he takes. How does this assuage his sense of complicity? Are there any other strategies he could have employed?

8. Mengele's pseudoscientific understanding of genetics was used to further the Nazi agenda. In general, what do you think the relationship between science and politics is? What responsibilities should scientists uphold with that relationship in mind?

9. One of the most gut-wrenching things Brasse documents is the forced sterilization of Jewish women. How were these procedures legitimized by the Nazi regime? Do you know of any other, comparable sterilization movements?

10. Can you pinpoint a single moment when Brasse decided to work actively against the SS? How do you think he overcame his fears?

11. Though at times Wilhelm Brasse was determined to forget everything about Auschwitz, his photos are a crucial tool in maintaining our historical memory of what happened there. Is it enough to remember? What more can we do to respect our history and avoid repeating it?

Picture Acknowledgments

The publisher would like to thank the following for kind permission to reproduce images:

  Wilhelm Brasse as a young man: copyright unknown
  Brasse in 1938: copyright unknown
  Brasse in 2009: Bartek Wrzesniowski/AFP via Getty Images
  Josef Mengele: Archival Collection of the Auschwitz-Birkenau State Museum in Oswiecim
  Carl Clauberg: Archival Collection of the Auschwitz-Birkenau State Museum in Oswiecim
  Maximilian Grabner: Archival Collection of the Auschwitz-Birkenau State Museum in Oswiecim
  Rudolf Friemel: Archival Collection of the Auschwitz-Birkenau State Museum in Oswiecim

Four Jewish girls: Archival Collection of the Auschwitz-Birkenau State Museum in Oswiecim

Jewish prisoners after alighting from a train: Yad Vashem Photo Archive, Jerusalem

Prisoner selection: Yad Vashem Photo Archive, Jerusalem

The sorting of personal belongings: Yad Vashem Photo Archive, Jerusalem

Czesława Kwoka: Archival Collection of the Auschwitz-Birkenau State Museum in Oswiecim

Krystyna Trzesniewska: Archival Collection of the Auschwitz-Birkenau State Museum in Oswiecim

Aron Loewi: Archival Collection of the Auschwitz-Birkenau State Museum in Oswiecim

Rozalia Kowalczyk: Archival Collection of the Auschwitz-Birkenau State Museum in Oswiecim

Women and children on their way to gas chamber number 4: Yad Vashem Photo Archive, Jerusalem

Jewish prisoners wait near gas chamber number 4: Yad Vashem Photo Archive, Jerusalem

Jozef Pysz: Archival Collection of the Auschwitz-Birkenau State Museum in Oswiecim

Unknown prisoner: Archival Collection of the Auschwitz-Birkenau State Museum in Oswiecim

Stefania Stiebler: Archival Collection of the Auschwitz-Birkenau State Museum in Oswiecim

Unknown Dutch political prisoner: Archival Collection of the Auschwitz-Birkenau State Museum in Oswiecim

Men in camp uniform: Yad Vashem Photo Archive, Jerusalem

Jewish women marching to their barracks: Yad Vashem Photo Archive, Jerusalem

Jewish women wearing camp uniform: Yad Vashem Photo Archive, Jerusalem

Gottlieb Wagner: Archival Collection of the Auschwitz-Birkenau State Museum in Oswiecim

Stanisław Watycha: Archival Collection of the Auschwitz-Birkenau State Museum in Oswiecim

Leo Israel Vogelbaum: Archival Collection of the Auschwitz-Birkenau State Museum in Oswiecim

August Wittek: Archival Collection of the Auschwitz-Birkenau State Museum in Oswiecim

Franz Slokau: Archival Collection of the Auschwitz-Birkenau State Museum in Oswiecim

About the Authors
and Translator

Luca Crippa is an expert in theology and philosophy. He has worked as a research professor and editorial consultant for many years. He is the author of a number of history textbooks and essays, historical novels, and documentaries.

Maurizio Onnis has traveled extensively in developing countries and has studied the anthropology and history of religions and cultures. He has written historical novels and screenplays.

Jennifer Higgins translates from French and Italian. Recent translations include *A Short Philosophy of Birds* by Philippe Dubois and Élise Rousseau and a cotranslation of *Faces on the Tip of My Tongue* by the contemporary French author Emmanuelle Pagnano, which was longlisted for the Man Booker International Prize 2020. She is also the program manager of the Oxford-based

Queen's College Translation Exchange, an initiative to develop an inspiring range of translation-related workshops and activities for schools, students, and the wider public.